Gaming the System

Gaming the System takes an active approach to learning about American government, using novel, exciting, and highly instructive games to help students learn politics by living it. These timeless games are the perfect complement to a core textbook in American government—covering key topics like the Constitution, the Supreme Court, Congress, political participation, campaigns and elections, the federal bureaucracy, the social contract, social movements, and public opinion—and can be applied to specific courses at other levels, as well.

For Instructors: These nine games are designed to be easily inserted into courses, with all but one fitting into one class session and all flexible enough to adapt or scale as needed. Games are designed so that students will be ready to play after minimal preparation and with little prior knowledge; instructors do not need to design or prepare any additional materials. An extensive instructor-only online resource provides everything needed to accompany each game:

- summary and discussion of the pedagogical foundations on active learning and games;
- instructions and advice for managing the game and staging under various logistical circumstances;
- student handouts and scoresheets, and more.

For Students: These games immerse participants in crucial narratives, build content knowledge, and improve critical thinking skills—at the same time providing an entertaining way to learn key lessons about American government. Each chapter contains complete instructions, materials, and discussion questions in a concise and ready-to-use form, in addition to time-saving tools like scorecards and 'cheat sheets.' The games contribute to course understanding, lifelong learning, and meaningful citizenship.

Alexander H Cohen is Assistant Professor of Political Science at Clarkson University in Potsdam, New York. He is an avid board and video gamer and regularly uses active learning in his classroom. His research interests include the effect of weather on political outcomes, institutional assessment, pedagogy, and zombies. His most recent book was entitled *Living with Zombies*.

John Alden is a social studies teacher in the Williamsburg Community School District in Iowa. He teaches 9th and 12th graders, covering the topics of geography and government. He earned his master's degree in social studies education from the University of Iowa, where he also met his coauthors.

Jonathan J. Ring is a lecturer in the Department of Political Science and a Global Security Fellow in the Baker Center for Public Policy at the University of Tennessee.

This is the classroom game book political science has been waiting for. In *Gaming the System*, authors Alexander H Cohen, John Alden, and Jonathan J. Ring neatly package a breadth of subfield exercises that test concepts, challenge students, and support active learning. This book gives time back to teachers hunting through learning activity haystacks, with every game easy to setup and distribute, and further tailorable to meet specific course objectives. Even better, each game has been rigorously playtested to assure educators that these games *work*. I wish I had this book years ago—a must-have for active learning classrooms.

> —Lt Col James "Pigeon" Fielder, Ph.D., Associate Professor of Political Science at the U.S. Air Force Academy, Manchester Games Studies Network research associate, and professional wargame design instructor

The book *Gaming the System: Nine Games to Teach American Government through Active Learning* provides a plethora of useful games and simulations for the effective teaching of American government that will engage students and allow them to discuss the activity of their classmates and themselves in a way that will create much richer and more productive classroom discussions and analysis.

> —**Victor Asal**, Professor of Political Science, SUNY Albany

Gaming the System

Nine Games to Teach American Government through Active Learning

Alexander H Cohen, John Alden, and Jonathan J. Ring

Routledge
Taylor & Francis Group

NEW YORK AND LONDON

First published 2020
by Routledge
52 Vanderbilt Avenue, New York, NY 10017

and by Routledge
2 Park Square, Milton Park, Abingdon, Oxon, OX14 4RN

*Routledge is an imprint of the Taylor & Francis Group,
an informa business*

Library of Congress Cataloging-in-Publication Data
A catalog record for this book has been requested

ISBN: 978-0-8153-8433-5 (hbk)
ISBN: 978-0-8153-8434-2 (pbk)
ISBN: 978-1-351-20451-4 (ebk)

Typeset in Sabon
by Apex CoVantage LLC

Visit the eResources: www.routledge.com/9780815384342

for anyone who has played Risk until dawn, the practice of strategy, and similar abstract concepts

for Phoebe, John, and Sarah

for the Larsons, Littaus, Rings, and Schilders

Contents

Preface

If you are an instructor who has adopted this text, we advise you to consult the online resources made available through the publisher for vital information (available at www.routledge. com/9780815384342). The published text you are now reading is for your students and so is important for you to read as well but is incomplete for your purposes. The resources online will help you to implement the games by providing content connections, logistical requirements, and valuable suggestions. The online resources also include essential scorekeeping tools and crucial handouts that by their nature could not be included in this volume.

Acknowledgments

The authors would like to thank all of the playtesters and colleagues who helped to make sure that these games work as intended. Special thanks go to students at Cleveland State University, Augustana College, the University of Tennessee, Knoxville, and in the Iowa City Community School District for playing the games. We would also like to thank Holly Robinson, Stacey Noble, our anonymous reviewers, and our fellow panel participants at the 2018 annual meeting of the Midwest Political Science Association for helping to improve these games.

We would additionally like to thank our families and pets who allowed us the many hours that we put into this book outside of the normal workday.

1 | Introduction

The Premise of the Book: Games and the Human Experience

We all played games when we were children. Whether it was Monopoly with the family, cribbage in study halls in high school, online games with friends, or simply inventing rules for make-believe at the playground, we have all—at some point in our lives—been captivated by gaming. Today legions of Americans continue to play games in their living rooms, in hobby shops, on their smart phones, and—yes—even in class.

Games are healthy. They help us learn about cooperation, competition, and compromise. They challenge us to think strategically and make tough decisions. They can stimulate our imagination and creativity and help us think critically about the world around us. Games are shared ways of making sense of the world. They are recursive; they transmit culture, norms, and values that shape us, just as we shape those aspects of humanity through gaming. And, most of all, a well-designed game can be a lot of fun.

We wrote this book because we believe that games, as a central part of the human experience, can have a central role in formal education as well. This book is a collection of games both grand and simple that are intended to stimulate an interest in political science, help teach important lessons, and make the classroom more enjoyable by making learning fun.

The Purpose of the Book: Learning Through Gaming

This book provides impactful educational games that enable learners to experience American politics rather than simply read about it. In these games, you will play as congresspersons, social activists, voters, and framers of the Constitution. Your experience will be rich and possibly complicated because each game tasks you with balancing priorities and making tough decisions, just like politics in the real world. This is no accident. The rules and mechanics of these games are drawn from actual challenges, negotiations, and struggles in US politics and society. It is our hope that the authentic nature of these games will help you to better understand the content of American politics and leave you with much to think about.

The games in this book, like the practice of politics, are also competitive. Politicians constantly jockey to get what they want, inevitably resulting in winners and losers. Our games reflect this reality by having players strive to obtain more resources, points, policy priorities, or movement victories than other players. Players in Chapter 4's Hard-Won Equality, for example, compete as different organizations within a broader social movement, seeking prestige for themselves while also trying to further the goals of the movement as a whole. This sort of realistic competition is not only authentic but also educational. The motivation engendered by competitive gaming stimulates learning and retention.

As much as we stress the authenticity of these games, though, they are not meant to duplicate reality. They are ways to play with reality to better understand it. In this sense, the games are not simulations. They do not replicate a historical event or process, nor are players ever asked to roleplay a particular historical figure. The games do, however, embody key ideas, questions, or challenges. The gameplay of Chapter 9's The Tragedy of the Lagoon exemplifies this starkly. In it, you play as lagoon monsters trying to survive, but this premise is almost inconsequential because the struggles that the monsters face are universal and easily applicable to US politics and society.

Why Games and Active Learning Work

Educational games like the ones found in this book are part of a broader approach to education called 'experiential learning' or 'active learning.' This style of teaching prioritizes student interaction and collaboration in the classroom. You have likely encountered various forms of active learning before, such as small group discussions, 'fishbowls,' 'think-pair-shares,' and other activities that have students investigating and analyzing topics together rather than passively digesting the content of an instructor's lecture or slideshow.

Some academic disciplines have thoroughly embraced active learning. Nursing is a good example (Bradley, 2006; Lasater, 2007). Intuitively, this makes sense. Nurses need significant content knowledge, but they also need to be able to access that knowledge in a wide variety of particular circumstances. Each patient is unique. Other disciplines, such as history, require significant content knowledge but do not face the same issues as nurses in needing to access that information in high stress situations. While active learning can still help teach historical content, it is not surprising that history programs use it less than nursing programs. In political science, we are arguably somewhere in between history and nursing programs in our using of active learning.

We have written this book because we think that political science should use active learning tools in the classroom more than it already does. Active learning works. For example, it helps students retain the information they encounter (Asal, 2005). Active learning gives students multiple ways to access and understand content. It puts them in a position where they can learn from each other, approach the content in their own way at their own pace, try out ideas, and build off of each other's strengths. All of this allows for deeper understanding and greater retention (Olson, 2012). Following from these findings, the games in the book encourage teamwork, negotiation, and collaboration that create mutual support networks among students to help them master the course's content. Our own research supports this as well.

Active learning has also been found to increase student motivation to learn (Petranek & Black, 1992; Asal, 2005). We witnessed this ourselves when testing the games. Students would often end the games fired up, having found new enthusiasm for the class and the content. Active learning also tends to boost learner confidence, which psychologists call 'self-efficacy' and is a big part of a person's motivation to learn (Shellman & Turan, 2006).

Finally, active learning is a good training ground for the post-college world. By emphasizing initiative, critical thinking, teamwork, and, yes, shaking students out of their 'comfort zone,' games can help prepare students for scenarios they will encounter in their future careers (Dougherty, 2003; Rackaway & Goertzen, 2008). Lectures can efficiently convey information, but they often do little to help students practice using the information they are encountering. Active learning works to solve this problem by having students use information much as they would in the workplace, such as in collaborative settings and on projects. The skills practiced in our games—critical thinking, strategizing, teamwork, negotiating, problem-solving, etc.—should be useful wherever you go after college. This book is consciously—and at times meticulously—designed to provide all these benefits to learners.

How to Get the Most Out of Games

Classroom Decorum

These games are competitive in nature, but there is no reason why they ought to be cutthroat. You will enjoy your experience the most if you accept victories graciously and losses with a smile. If you find yourself becoming so invested in a game that you are becoming angry or frustrated, it is time to take a step back and remember that this is just a learning tool like any other.

Preparation

Most of these games cannot be successfully played unless you read games ahead of time and prepare a basic strategy prior to the class in which the game is scheduled. Consult your instructor if you have questions about this. While the games in this book vary in complexity, few can be picked up entirely on the fly. If you spend twenty minutes reading a game while it is in progress, you are sure not only to lose but also to lose badly. Most students spend some time thinking critically about possible strategies, forming alliances, and considering opening moves well in advance of the game, and while these are not guarantors of success, they will certainly help you along. Reading the evening or morning before a game is good practice.

The Public Space

While playing your game, be sure to pay attention to the Public Space. The Public Space is utilized in virtually every game as a central place to display and update information relevant to the game. The exact nature of the Public Space will be determined by your instructor: it may be a whiteboard, a projected Excel file, or even something of their creation. No matter its form, though, the Public Space will contain vital strategic information necessary for you to succeed. Use it to make strategic decisions about your opponents, evaluate your own possible decisions, and try to predict what might happen next.

The Golden Rule: Your Instructor Runs the Show

The most important thing to keep in mind as you read this book is that no matter what is written in a chapter, your instructor has the final say in resolving disputes, interpreting rules, or even changing them. There are a number of reasons for this. Different instructors may use the same game to teach different lessons, depending upon the focus of your class, and so they may tweak rules accordingly. They may also opt to change the timing of rounds or make sudden adjustments to rules. Remember that when your instructor does such things, they do them for good reasons, so do recognize that they run the classroom, not this text. Listen to them.

The Rest of the Book

In the following chapters, you will find nine games, most of which should take about forty-five minutes to play (though instructors have the ability to lengthen or shorten them), as well as a collection of shorter games in the final chapter. In Chapter 2, Signing the Social Contract, you will find yourself in a fictional state of nature and must consider the central question of whether you need a government. Your initial situation is grim and illustrates the distressing conundrums inherent to surviving in an uncertain world. You have to gather enough resources to survive both today and in the future while weighing the merits of going it alone, grouping up, or even stealing from a neighbor. As the rounds of the game progress, you will interact through structured exchanges to advance up the ladder of civilization toward government, but not all may like the idea of a sovereign. The winners will be those who gather the most resources, whether under the protection of a state or through the freedom of the state of nature.

Chapter 3, A More Perfect Union, will take you to the 1787 Constitutional Convention, where you will serve as a delegation from a given state. Your goal is to re-sculpt Madison's initial proposal for the Constitution in your favor. To do so, you are given objectives and provided with rules of debate and amendment. Massachusetts, for instance, desires representation to be apportioned on the basis of population, while Georgia seeks the opposite. However, as with the Constitution, the document can only be ratified by three-fourths of the delegations, making it very difficult to assemble a final document without forcing you to make compromises in your initial strategies. It may be quite difficult for three-fourths of the states to agree on one version of the Constitution, and so students will be pressed to negotiate carefully across several well-defined policy areas, just like the actual delegates in 1787. The game's winner is the delegation that achieves the most points through seeing your objectives represented in a final ratified document.

Chapter 4 brings you Hard-Won Equality. This game conveys the instrumental struggles faced by social movement organizations pursuing legal equality in the United States. Students will work in small groups to create and implement a strategy for a hypothetical social movement organization modeled after key elements of the Women's Rights Movement of the 1920s and the Civil Rights Movement of the 1960s. You will spend finite resources on tactics such as protests, lobbying, and public outreach to overcome the myriad obstacles you encounter while pushing for change in a rigged system. Along the way, you will grapple with tough questions about equality, rights, and civic engagement in a democracy.

Chapter 5, Nomination Scrimmage, explores electoral politics through a hypothetical contest between five imaginary Republican candidates on Super Tuesday. To succeed, you will need to carefully determine your candidate's ideological dispositions and policy positions and then campaign among an ideologically diverse set of states that feature different rules of apportioning representatives. Successful resource management and an eye for strategy are crucial to beating the other candidates who are after the same goal as you: the Republican nomination for president.

Chapter 6 delves into lawmaking. Written by Committee is set in a heated conference committee formed to resolve disagreements between the Senate and House versions of a bill. The game will be a whirlwind microcosm of lawmaking in which you, a legislator, will succeed based on how closely the compromise bill the committee creates matches your own preferences. You will be able to wheel and deal, bribe and spy, and win favor with constituents and interest groups based on what you accomplish in the committee. No one will get everything they want in this game, but the lawmaker who comes closest wins.

In A Best-Case Scenario, found in Chapter 7, you will quest to reach the highest court in the land and prevail there. You will act as lawyers for the plaintiff in a landmark case that serves as the narrative backbone of the gameplay. You will attempt to make correct choices as you move your case toward the Supreme Court. In order to win, you must seek an expedient path to the Supreme Court and do your best to convince at least five of the nine justices to take your side. Along the way, you will need to use your knowledge of the US judicial system to avoid setbacks that can cost the unprepared their shot at victory.

Chapter 8 offers Agency and Oversight. At stake are the relative powers of the executive and legislative branches of the government in this tug of war over how much independence federal bureaucrats should have. You will play as either a government agency or a congressional committee tasked with monitoring an agency. These institutions want different things and try to outdo each other in a principal–agent interaction that results in lots of opportunities for both conflict and compromise. The negotiated outcomes that agencies and committees reach yield political capital, which can in turn be spent strategically to improve one's standing in the public's eye and move players that much closer to victory.

In Chapter 9, The Tragedy of the Lagoon, you will be torn between profit and cooperation in this economic battle royal. The fictional premise of the game puts you in the role of lagoon monsters who have to make tough choices as they try to survive and thrive in their watery home. Each turn you take actions that allow you to profit, avoid personal dangers, or protect collective resources like fish and water. The high opportunity costs of these different actions allow the game to illustrate important concepts in the social sciences like the tragedy of the commons, freeriding, collective action, and economic goods. The game also supports lessons related to environmental policy and interest groups. The winner of the game will be the group who can best balance their own pursuit of wealth with avoiding the hazards that lie in wait for these industrious lagoon monsters.

In Chapter 10, The People Have Spoken, groups of students have a short time to adopt the name, persona, and symbols of a real-world interest group. Each group encounters and responds to a randomized series of events and must capitalize on these opportunities by delivering a creative and effective political message to sway public opinion. The game illustrates how public opinion develops and how what is popular may not necessarily be what is most honest or objective.

Finally, Chapter 11's Game Goulash offers a collection of games designed to run about twenty minutes. These games cover topics like political participation, 'first past the post' elections, the median voter, public opinion polling, caucuses, and the media. They are useful as lesson supplements and as means of 'chunking' lessons to break the monotony of a lecture. And watch out for Squidfolk.

Works Cited

Asal, V. (2005). Playing games with international relations. *International Studies Perspectives*, 6(3), 359–373.

Bradley, P. (2006). The history of simulation in medical education and possible future directions. *Medical Education*, 40(3), 254–262.

Dougherty, B. (2003). Byzantine politics: Using simulations to make sense of the Middle East. *PS: Political Science and Politics*, 36(2), 239–244.

Jefferson, K. (1999). The Bosnian war crimes trial simulation: Teaching students about the fuzziness of world politics and international law. *PS: Political Science and Politics*, 32, 589–592.

Lasater, K. (2007). High-fidelity simulation and the development of clinical judgement: Students' experiences. *Journal of Nursing Education*, 46(6).

Olson, K. (2012). Making it real: Using a collaborative simulation to teach crisis communications. *Journal on Excellent in College Teaching*, 23(2), 25–47.

Petranek, C., & Black, R. (1992). Three levels of learning in simulations: Participating, debriefing, and journal writing. *Simulation and Gaming*, *23*(2), 174–185.

Rackaway, C., & Goertzen, B. (2008). Debating the future: A social security political leadership simulation. *Journal of Political Science Education*, *4*, 330–340.

Shellman, S. M., & Turan, K. (2006). Do simulations enhance student learning? An empirical evaluation of an IR simulation. *Journal of Political Science Education*, *2*(1), 19–32.

Smith, E., & Boyer, M. (1996). Designing in-class simulations. *PS: Political Science and Politics*, *29*(4), 690–694.

2

Signing the Social Contract

A Game About the State of Nature

Overview

In this activity, you will play as a person lost and alone in an anarchic setting (meaning there is no government to protect or oppress you). The game might take place long after an apocalypse or long before civilization ever formed. Regardless, your life is hard and lonesome. You struggle to find enough resources to survive, and you are left with hard choices about whether to scavenge, steal from others, or hide what little you have. Your goal is to maximize your chances of survival by gathering the most resources, but this will be difficult to achieve because every other player shares this same goal.

This struggle is premised on what philosophers call social contract theory. Philosophers like Thomas Hobbes and John Locke were troubled with the question of why a person should prefer to have a government instead of being without one. That is, they wondered why a person would want to 'sign the social contract' and agree to give up some of their freedoms to be ruled by laws. To find an answer, these seventeenth-century intellectuals proposed a thought experiment. In this case, Hobbes and Locke both proposed what we call a 'state of nature,' a fictional setting in which people live with no government whatsoever. The philosophers used this thought experiment to consider several important questions. Would people in this condition be willing to give up some of their independence in return for greater security? Would they be able to overcome mistrust and fear of each other to work together? Would a person without a government choose to join one of their own free will? Hobbes and Locke thought that the answers to all three of these questions was ultimately 'yes.' They consequently argued that having a government was better than not having one. We want you to find your own answers, though, and so we have turned the state of nature into a game. As you play, we hope you will think about the questions in this paragraph that prompted the original thought experiment.

Instructions and Rules

Gameplay

Core Concepts and Actions

In this game, the provisions you need to survive, prosper, and overcome opponents—things like food, water, clothing, weapons, tools, etc.—are all measured as one concept: 'Resources.' Your goal is not just to gain Resources but also to have more than other players so that you are relatively safe from their attacks. This means that by the end of the game, you want to have the highest number of Resources. You start the game with only a small number of Resources, though, and this starting sum is determined randomly by your instructor. You will keep track of Resource gains and losses through your Personal Ledger, which is something that your instructor will give you at the start of the game. Your initial Resources will be indicated in the 'Round 1 Starting Resources' cell of this Ledger. Be sure to keep your Resource total secret unless a game mechanic requires sharing it with another player. Later in the game, you will also receive a Group Ledger. Both Ledgers are explained further in these instructions, so read on!

For your convenience, both examples of both Ledgers are provided below in Tables 2.1 and 2.2.

TABLE 2.1 Personal Ledger

Round Number	Starting Resources	Action	Ending Resources
1			
2			
3			
4—Kin Groups now allowed			
5			
6			
7			
8—Communities now allowed			
9			
10			
11			
12—Government now allowed			
13			
14			
15			
16			
17			
18			
19			

Possible Actions—Quick Reference

Gather: Write a **G** in your Personal Ledger in the Action column for this round. At the end of the round, you'll add Resources to your stockpile. If you're in a group, you'll earn even more.

Steal: Write an **S** in your Personal Ledger in the Action column for this round. If you have more Resources than someone you Steal from, you get their Resources. But if they have more than you, they get yours. You do not designate who you are Stealing from when writing in the Action column.

Hide: Write an **H** in your Personal Ledger in the Action column for this round. Gain no Resources this round and become immune to Stealing.

Join: Write a **J** and the name of the group you are joining in your Personal Ledger in the Action column for this round. Group members must vote unanimously to include you.

Defend: Write a **D** in your Personal Ledger in the Action column for this round. You can stop one Steal action used against a member of your group (including, if necessary, yourself). Defend can only be used if you are in a group. It can only be used by a fixed number of players in your group—for every four group members, you have one Defender.

TABLE 2.2 Group Ledger

Round Number	Total Ending Resources	Group Members	Shares per Member (Ending Resources Divided by Group Members)
4—Kin Groups now allowed			
5			
6			
7			
8—Communities now allowed			
9			
10			
11			
12—Government now allowed			
13			
14			
15			
16			
17			
18			
19			

Additional Considerations

Each group has the ability to designate one Defender per every four members.
In Kin and Community Groups, Gathering yields two Resources.
In Governments, Gathering yields three Resources.

In each round of the game, you will take one action that can increase, protect, or share your Resources. You will take your one action per round at the same time that the other players take theirs. To coordinate all of this activity, you will write your chosen action in your Ledger. You write this action in the Action column of your Ledger described below.

The possible actions you can take include:

1. **Gather:** Write a **G** in your Personal Ledger in the Action column for this round. This means that you are devoting your time to

gathering food, farming, mining, or doing something else that yields Resources. At the end of the round, you will add one Resource to your stockpile. If you are in a group, you will earn even more.

2. **Steal:** Write an *S* in your Personal Ledger in the Action column for this round. This means that you are using brute force to try to take Resources from another player. Stealing can be a gamble. If you have more Resources than someone you Steal from, you get their Resources. But if they have more than you, they get yours. You do not designate from whom you are Stealing when writing in the Action column; this choice comes a bit later. A more detailed explanation is available in the 'Sequence of Play' section below.

3. **Hide:** Write an *H* in your Personal Ledger in the Action column for this round. Gain no Resources this round and become immune to Stealing.

4. **Join:** Write a *J and* the name of the group you are joining in your Personal Ledger in the Action column for this round. The Join action is used whether you are forming a group from scratch with other players, joining an already existing group as an individual, moving between groups, or merging existing groups into a larger one. Note that groups cannot be formed until round 4, and so you cannot use the Join action until then. Additionally, all members of a group must agree to include you for the Join action to succeed.

5. **Defend:** Write a *D* in your Personal Ledger in the Action column for this round. This means you are devoting your time to protecting your group. You must be in a group to use it. You can stop one Steal action used against a member of your group (including, if necessary, yourself). The Thief's Steal action simply does not happen, and the Thief returns to her or his seat. It can only be used by a fixed number of players in your group—for every four group members, you can designate one Defender.

All of these actions will be discussed in greater detail in the 'Sequence of Play' section below. Please read that section closely to gain a sense of how your instructor is likely to conduct the game.

Before we turn to that description, though, there are a few more things we wish to note about groups and invalid actions.

Groups

Joining and forming groups can be an important part of the game. Grouping up reflects players being willing to trust each other and work together for collective security. This idea of trust is represented mechanically in the game by having players in groups pool their Resources. The collective security aspect is found in a new action that groups have called 'Defend.' Forming a group is therefore a tradeoff. Players who use the Join action abandon some of their freedom in return for enhanced security and teamwork. It is up to you to gauge whether this tradeoff is worth it for you. In our experience, players have done well alone and in groups, meaning that deciding whether or not to Join a group is a genuine and important choice in this game.

Groups become available at round 4, and at rounds 8 and 12, new possibilities for the group action are unlocked. Players can form the smallest size of groups for the first time in round 4 (called Kin Groups), form even larger groups in round 8 (called Communities), and create the largest size of group in round 12 (called Governments). All of this is done with the Join action. Players who wish to Join or form a group simply write a *J* followed by their group's name in the Ledger for their action that round, such as '*J*—The Fighting Mongooses.' When Joining a group, players give their personal wealth to the group, which then redistributes it to all members in equitable 'shares' in a process described below.

Kin Groups, Communities, and Governments differ in a few ways. The primary difference is the number of players in each type of group. The minimum and maximum sizes of the group types will be calculated by your instructor before the game starts and displayed for the class in the Public Space. Unless your instructor otherwise designates so, a Kin Group holds between 10% and 20% of the players in the game. Communities hold between 20.1% and 40% of players. Governments hold between 40.1% and 80%. The exact values for your class may vary, though, based on instructor preferences. Group sizes cannot grow beyond their maximum value until the next highest group type is unlocked (see Box 2.1 for an example). If an existing group shrinks below that minimum value, they either become the next lowest group type or, if they are already a Kin Group, simply stay a Kin Group (albeit a small one).

Box 2.1 Example of How Groups Work

There are 25 students in the class, and it is round 7. The maximum number of members in a Kin Group is five (Kin Groups may hold 10%–20% of the total number of students in the class, and 20% of twenty-five is five). The group 'UnLocked' contains five people. Betty wants to Join 'UnLocked,' but cannot, because this would make 'UnLocked' contain six people. The next round, round 8, unlocks Communities. The new maximum numbers of members in a group rises to ten, and so Betty can now Join 'UnLocked,' so long as the members of 'UnLocked' agree.

Another difference between group types relates to the Defend action. As described above, this action lets the player who uses it stop one Steal action taken against a member of his or her group. For every four members in a group, one member can choose to use the Defend action each round. So, a group with thirteen members could have up to three Defenders in a round.

Finally, being in a group enables you to Gather more efficiently, reflecting the increased utility of communal living. Players in Kin and Community Groups will Gather two Resources, and a player in a Government will Gather three Resources.

Invalid Actions

Actions that violate the game's rules are invalid. If the instructor decides that one of your actions was invalid, you must cross it out in your Personal Ledger and lose your action for that round. If the instructor determines that you have wrongfully gained Resources from an invalid action in any round (past or current), the instructor, at their sole discretion, may alter your current balance of

Resources. Likewise, if the instructor determines that other individuals or groups may have wrongfully lost Resources due to the invalid actions of others, they may compensate them by altering their balance of Resources. All of this applies to both Group and Individual Ledgers.

Sequence of Play

Some actions occur before others in a round out of necessity. If everyone tried to perform their action at once, the game would become chaotic. To avoid this, each round follows a standardized format. It is important that you listen to your instructor as rounds begin and are resolved. This is the sequence of play for each round:

1. **Round Start:** The instructor announces the start of the round.
2. **Actions Are Entered:** Players have a specified time to discuss choosing actions, forming groups, Joining groups, determining who might Defend within a group, etc. The time limit for this is set by the instructor at the start of the game and will be known to all. During this phase of the game, players may move around the room and communicate freely. By the conclusion of this phase, all players must record their actions in their Personal Ledgers.
3. **Players Rise:** The instructor calls when the time allotted for entering actions has elapsed. All players stand to signal that they are ready. By this time, all players must have selected an action and recorded it in their Personal Ledger in the Action column. Any player who has not yet recorded an action will not get to use their action, but they can still be affected by the actions of others, such as Stealing.
4. **Thieves Select Targets:** Players who wish to Steal move next to their intended target. They do not have to have designated *who* they will Steal from until this point (all that they have written in their Ledger is 'S').

   a. All Thieves raise their hands to indicate that they are Stealing. Thieves may Steal from anyone, including other Thieves. Multiple Thieves may not select the same target.

   b. A Thief selects a target by walking to a victim and stating, "I'm stealing from you." The victim raises both of their hands to indicate that they are targeted for Stealing. Once a victim is designated, no other Thief may target that victim. The Thief then lowers his or her hand to show that they have selected their target. When all Thieves have lowered their hands, the targets lower their hands too.

c. Any players who chose to Defend may move next to a targeted player who is a member of their group. This individual is protected from a Steal action originating from a Thief of the Defender's choice. That Thief's attempt is aborted and no Resources are exchanged. Remember, each group can only use one Defender per every four people in their group.

d. If a Thief has attempted to Steal from someone who is Hiding, the Hide action is revealed. The Thief does not gain or lose Resources, and the Hiding player retains their own Resources.

e. If a Steal action is not Defended against and the victim is not Hiding, both the Thief and the target reveal their Resources to each other. Whoever has the higher Resource total takes all of the other player's Resources and adds that sum to his or her own. If there is a tie, nothing happens; both players retain their Resources. The results are recorded in the 'Ending Resources' column of the Personal Ledger that corresponds to the current round. Note that when updating Resource tallies, players watch one another update their tally sheets to ensure that everyone is playing honestly.

f. If a Thief targets a Thief who is in turn targeting another Thief, the *last* Thief to designate a target Steals first. In Figure 2.1 below, Thieves are numbered by the order in which they reached their targets:

This 'Thief Chain' would be resolved the following way:

- Thief 3 unsuccessfully Steals from Thief 2. Thief 3 loses all Resources; Thief 2 now has twelve Resources.

- Thief 2 is unable to Steal from Thief 1 because Thief 1 is protected by a Defender. Note that Thief 1 is part of the Defender's group. Thief 2 retains twelve Resources.

- The Gatherer then loses their Resources to Thief 1, who has four Resources, more than the Gatherer's two.

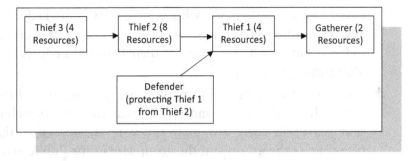

Figure 2.1 Thief Chain

g. If you have lost all your Resources, do not worry! This is normal, and there are plenty of ways to recover.

5. **Gathering:** Players update their personal Resource tallies in the 'Ending Resources' column of their Personal Ledger based on Gather actions. Gathering increases a player's Resource total by one if that player is not in a group. Remember that being in groups of various sizes affects Gathering. In a Kin and Community Group, Gathering yields two Resources; in Governments, it yields three.

6. **Personal Ledgers Are Finalized:** By now, Thieves, their targets, and Gatherers, as well as those Joining new groups, have properly updated the 'Ending Resources' column of their Personal Ledgers. However, some players may have taken other options that do not change this total, such as Joining or Hiding. At this point, *all* players should properly update their 'Ending Resources' column, if they have not done so already.

7. **Group Joining:** Players who have recorded the Join action resolve this now.

a. The instructor asks if any group of players are Joining a *new* group (in effect, creating a group). Remember, the group size must meet the minimum threshold for the corresponding group type, as indicated in the Public Space. If the new group is formed, the group provides the instructor with a name for the group, and the group name and its size (number of members) are recorded on the Public Space. The group designates a Bookkeeper, who is given a Group Ledger to update in addition to his or her Personal Ledger. It is crucial that students continue to update their Personal Ledgers even after forming a group.

b. The instructor asks if any players are joining an *existing* group. If so, the group must vote unanimously to include that player in their group. If the vote is successful, that player joins the group and the group size in the Public Space is updated accordingly. If not, the player's Join action is wasted.

   i. Note: A player in one group can opt to Join another group. Players leaving a group take whatever Resources are in the Ending Resources column of their Personal Ledger at the time of their departure.

c. The number of individuals in each group is counted. The status of groups as Kin Group, Community Group, or Government are updated at this time. Remember, groups cannot exceed the size necessary to form a Community group until round 8, or a Government until round 12.

8. **Bookkeepers Update Group Ledgers:**

a. If a new group has just been formed, players forming a group sum their individual Resource tallies into one sum. This is recorded in the Total Ending Resources column of the Group Ledger. The number of players in the group is recorded in the Group Members column.

b. In existing groups, the Bookkeeper sums all individual Resources into the Total Ending Resources box of the Group Ledger.

c. All groups (new and existing) recalculate the shares of Resources allotted to each player. The Bookkeeper in each group divides the number in the Total Ending Resources box by the number of members in the group (the Group Members column), including those who have just joined but not any who have just left, and records this in the Shares per Member box of the Group Ledger.

9. **Starting Resources Set for Next Round:** All players calculate the contents of the Starting Resource column for the next round on the *next* row of their Personal Ledger.

   a. For players not in a group, this is simply the same number of Resources held at the end of the last round.

   b. For players in a group, it is their personal share of the overall group's Resources, designated in the 'Individual Share' box of the Group Ledger.

10. **End of Round:** The instructor announces that all tallies have been completed and the next round begins (go to Step One).

The Public Space

To see an example of a sample Public Space, please see Table 2.3:

TABLE 2.3 Public Space for Signing the Social Contract

Total Number of Students in Class:	25

	Minimum Players	Maximum Players	Round Available	Group Names	# of Members
Kin Groups	3	5	4	The Sad Pandas	3
Communities	6	10	8	The Angry Bees	3
Governments	11	20	12		

Round Number:	4

Scoring

At the end of round 20 or at a time designated by the instructor, final scores are calculated. An ungrouped player's score is equal to their Ending Resource total, shown in the Ending Resources box. A grouped player's score is equal to their group's average Resource share at the end of the final round. If an individual player has the highest score, he or she is the winner. If a group's members have the highest score, they are all the winners.

Debriefing

Describing What Happened

1. Suppose that you have to describe the game you played to someone who did not see it. What would you say to best describe it?

2. What were the three most significant events in the game?

3. What are four adjectives that you would use to describe the state of nature in the game?

4. Did the game end the way you expected? Why or why not?

5. What did you decide to do with your first move? Knowing what you know now, would you have played the game any differently?

Relating the Game to the World

6. Identify a situation from the real world that is like the one portrayed in the game. How are the situations similar? How are they different?

7. If the game continued to run for an infinite number of rounds, what would the outcome be? Is this a realistic model of the growth of human civilization?

8. Think about the role of Defender. Give an example of a Defender in modern life.

9. Think about the role of Thieves. Give an example of a Thief in modern life.

10. What was a major turning point in the game, and why did it alter the course of the game? Identify one major historical event that it resembles.

Thinking Deeply

11. What was the best strategy for gaining Resources and winning the game? Using a hypothetical group of humans struggling to survive but *without* using terms from the game (like Gatherers, Thieves, Groups, etc.), explain what this strategy would actually look like.

12. How did not being able to see other players' Resource levels affect your choice of actions?

13. If you had to guess based on the game, would you say that getting people to cooperate together and form a shared government is difficult or easy? Why?

14. Based on your experiences in the game, are human beings more predisposed to conflict or cooperation?

15. Think about the size of your class. How would the game have been different if the class were very big or very small? How might this observation help those in power facilitate cooperation in the real world?

Creating New Ideas

16. Suppose that your class was transported to an uninhabited island with no hope of rescue.

    a. What do you think would happen over the course of the first 60 days on the island?

    b. If you could choose, what sort of government would you want your class to have (i.e., democratic, communist, authoritarian, etc.)? Why?

    c. What rules would you want your government to have to make sure that life on the island stays peaceful?

    d. What are two lessons that you would take from the game that you would wish to apply to life on the deserted island?

17. If you could change the game in one way to teach another lesson about human nature, how would you change it?

3

A More Perfect Union

A Game About the Constitutional Convention

Overview

The year is 1787. Despite having achieved their independence from Great Britain, the thirteen former colonies—now called 'states'—face an uncertain future. They sit in the loose alliance established by the Articles of Confederation. The Articles give each state a great deal of independence while leaving the national government of the US relatively weak. The Continental Congress, which is the legislature of the national government, has very little authority over the states. While this arrangement was effective in defeating the British during the Revolutionary War, weaknesses in the system are becoming painfully apparent now that independence has been achieved.

States often disagree and fail to cooperate on important issues. They are not working together to supply troops to defend the country. The national government lacks the power to impose taxes to pay for armies and lacks the ability to recruit troops itself. This leaves the United States' ability to defend itself in serious doubt. Threats on the United States' borders are another concern. Even though Spain fought on the side of the Americans during the rebellion, Spanish fortresses and troops remain in Florida, near

America's borders. Some wonder whether Spain wants the US's territory. Indigenous groups are also becoming more and more unhappy as colonists continue to push inland. The British, who still harbor designs to reclaim their lost colonies, maintain a strong military presence in Canada and have overwhelming naval superiority. A lack of money in the national treasury is also a growing problem. The Continental Congress owes massive amounts of money to both the Dutch and the French, from whom they had borrowed during the war. This, combined with the inability to impose taxes, makes it difficult for the government to pay for the things it wants to do, including pay the wages of its soldiers. In fact, just four years earlier in 1783, George Washington barely managed to prevent his own troops from mutinying when the Continental Congress could not agree to authorize their back pay. With the states divided, no national government strong enough to unite them, and so many pressing problems, the future looks bleak indeed.

For these reasons, the Continental Congress has authorized a special meeting in Philadelphia, Pennsylvania, to revise the Articles of Confederation. This meeting—called the Constitutional Convention—quickly takes on a life of its own as representatives from twelve of the thirteen states began the task of crafting the Constitution. In this game, you (individually or as a group, depending on the size of your class) will serve as one of these states' delegations. Your objective is to help craft a Constitution that meets the unique political needs of your state. You will be provided with clear objectives, but the path to meeting those objectives is up to you. You will need to bargain, negotiate, deceive, and compromise with your fellow delegates to build a Constitution that works for *you*, as measured by a score calculated at the end of the game. This is not easy work: coalitions will rise and fall as delegates attempt to optimize their score, and most delegations will keep their goals secret as they jockey for position. Importantly, the language of the Constitution must be approved by your fellow delegations, so the process of writing and editing the Constitution will take more than one draft, with plenty of back-and-forth. The final draft for the Constitution must be ratified by three-fourths of the states in the Union. Some states may withhold support for the Constitution until their political objectives are met; others are eager to embrace a new political order but only under certain terms. You must navigate these treacherous waters to do the best you can for the people of your state.

Significantly, this game is not intended to provide a step-by-step recreation of all aspects of the Convention. In order to ensure smooth gameplay, many historical elements of the Convention have been deliberately omitted or modified. Parliamentary procedure is drastically simplified. Students working together within state delegations cooperate to secure objectives. This is quite different from the historical delegations to the Convention. Within those groups of men there were often disagreements, big personalities, and absences that would be too distracting and counterproductive to replicate in the game. Consequently, we have unified each delegation internally, giving common goals to all delegates from a state. This allows delegations to focus on what matters most: strategically pursuing their state's interests. All state delegations are also assumed to have arrived at the Convention at the same time, which was historically not the case (bad roads and long distances meant that many arrived late). To rein in the potentially infinite scope of issues available for discussion, the game focuses on only the most salient issues and sets aside many of the more stylistic or substantively esoteric issues discussed. Rhode Island, which did not attend the Convention, is included to provide an important perspective and because it was part of the ratification process. Finally, the ratification process itself will take place by a vote of states at the Convention; in reality, the ratification process stretched on for many months and took place after exhaustive debate in the state legislatures.

Instructions and Rules

Gameplay

During a session prior to the game, your instructor will divide you into thirteen delegations of roughly equal size. If your class is small, some delegations may consist of only one student, or there may be fewer than thirteen delegations. This is entirely normal and does not advantage any state or affect the balance of the game. The instructor will distribute a State Briefing handout to each delegation. These State Briefings provide important information about the state that group represents. You will see some background information about your state, its historical delegation, your suggested strategy at the Convention, your position on six specific questions (more on this later) and one or more 'Pet Projects.' Read this information carefully, and do not share it with other groups (for reasons apparent soon).

On the day of the game, delegations should sit far enough apart from one another so that no group can eavesdrop on any other, or, worse still, peek at their materials! Think of this physical location in the classroom as your 'home base'—a place where delegations can go to find you, if you are not otherwise engaged in meetings.

Your instructor will place the current proposed version of the Constitution on the classroom whiteboard, blackboard, or projector, which here—like all games—is called the Public Space. This text resembles the Virginia Plan brought forward by James Madison. This is the text you will be revising throughout this game.

In this game, the Virginia Plan consists of answers to six important questions about the Constitution. Over the course of the simulation, delegations will attempt to change the answers to these questions in order to increase their score, which is described on your State Briefings (again, more on this later). The numbered items should be written in the Public Space by your instructor at the start of the game, as they appear here. The initial answers to those questions, which are subject to revision over the course of the game, are listed below. Next, explanatory notes, which appear below numbered text, are here for reference and are not placed in the Public Space.

1. Should the states be bound in a permanent Union under a government that can wage war?

- Initial Answer: Yes.
- This answer must be 'yes' in order to proceed with a ratification vote. If the Constitution is not ratified, this becomes a 'no' for the purposes of scoring. This establishes a strong central government that can conduct foreign affairs, raise an army, and declare war.

2. Should the national legislature have the power to tax?

- Initial Answer: Yes.
- This is a major source of power and makes for a more powerful national government.

3. How should representation in that legislature be apportioned?

- Initial Answer: On the basis of population.
- Apportionment refers to the way that population is converted to political representation. Madison proposed that each person in each state be counted when determining the number of representatives apportioned (like our current House of Representatives). Small states argued that all states should receive the same number of representatives (like our current Senate).

4. Should a chief executive exist and how should this executive be selected?

- Initial Answer: Yes, and they should be selected by the legislature.
- Another way to think about this question is: how powerful should the president be? Some would say 'powerful,' which would require making the chief executive independent of the legislature, so that the chief executive would not be subject to recall or disciplines. This would mean allowing 'the people' to elect the chief executive. Others suggested that the chief executive should be weak, which would mean making the job dependent on legislative approval.

5. Should slaves count as people for the purposes of apportionment?

- Initial Answer: No position.
- If question 3. above does not involve apportionment on the basis of population, then the answer to this question is automatically set to 'no' for the purposes of scoring. After all, if all states are represented equally in the legislature, then counting slaves does not matter. Southern states want their slaves to be counted as people in order to increase their representation in government; Northern states are skeptical of this approach as it would empower Southern states. Note

that this question is not about whether slavery should be legal or not.

6. Should the importation of slaves be permitted?

- Initial Answer: No position.
- During the time of the Constitutional Convention, just a handful of Southern states were permitting the importation of new slaves from lands abroad.

To help you visualize what this might look like, a sample Public Space is provided in Table 3.1:

TABLE 3.1 Initial Public Space

Question	Answer
1 Should the states be bound in a permanent Union under a government that can wage war?	Yes.
2 Should the national legislature have the power to tax?	Yes.
3 How should representation in that legislature be apportioned?	On the basis of population.
4 Should a chief executive exist and how should this executive be selected?	Yes, and they should be selected by the legislature.
5 Should slaves count as people for the purposes of apportionment?	No opinion.
6 Should the importation of slaves be permitted?	No opinion.

Additional Information for Pet Projects
The capital of the United States shall be in New York City, New York.
Any escaped slave captured must be returned to their owner.

Sequence of Play

Once you have had an opportunity to review your State Briefing and the Virginia Plan is recorded in the Public Space, the Convention can begin. You or your group will want to spend some time studying your State Briefings carefully and map out an initial strategy, keeping in mind that to win, your strategy must be fluid and reactive to the actions of other states. During the Convention, you and your group members are free to move around the room and discuss whatever you please with other states. Likely, you will spend some time noting state positions on other issues, perhaps making friends, and getting a sense for what proposals might be palatable to the larger group. These discussions take place informally and may take place in secret (such that other states are excluded from your meetings or conversations). Because you are under no obligation to be truthful about your objectives (and may have incentives to be less than honest at times), you should not share your goal sheets with anyone outside of your group. Guard them preciously.

As stated above, conversations between states are informal ways to consider proposals. However, there are two formal actions that you can take at any time. These actions are (1) amending the Virginia Plan and (2) moving to ratify.

Amending the Virginia Plan

At any time, any state may propose altering the answers to the listed questions—in other words, propose altering the draft of the Constitution—by standing before the Public Space and informing the instructor that they are 'taking the floor.' The instructor will call a halt to deliberation and direct the class's attention to the delegation proposing the change. The delegation that has taken the floor can propose two sorts of changes to the draft: altering existing answers or adding new components to the Constitution by writing them in a designated space, which may satisfy Pet Projects (see below). The delegation may propose multiple changes at once. Proposing a single change can be an expedient way to move toward accomplishing a goal, while proposing multiple changes at once is a good way to get buy-in from many states, provided that these changes have already been informally negotiated between states. When doing so, the delegation making the proposal may accompany the proposal with a brief persuasive speech lasting no longer than one minute. Delegations are free to propose *any* language that supports their strategy, but may not alter the initial questions—only the answers. Some language may only partially satisfy a delegation's goals. Scoring is explained in the section below.

Once the proposing delegation has clearly outlined the changes it proposes to make, it must 'move to amend' the Constitution accordingly. Then, another delegation must 'second' the proposal by stating 'seconded.' If the motion is not seconded, it dies and no changes are made. If the motion is seconded, all delegations vote on the proposed changes. Delegations may ask questions about the changes to ensure that they are clear on what they are voting on, and the proposing delegation may choose to sketch potential language in the Public Space to establish clarity if needed. Voting is done through a show of hands, but be sure that each delegation only votes once! If a simple majority (seven states when thirteen states are playing) votes for the changes, the old language is replaced with the new language. If a majority does not vote in favor of the changes, the old language remains.

Here are a few important things to keep in mind when proposing and voting on changes. First, the proposal must be voted on in totality and not broken into individual pieces. So, if a state proposes to alter the answers to questions 2, 3, and 4, the Convention cannot approve just 3 and 4. In other words, any motion that includes multiple changes is a package deal. Thus, when proposing changes, states must carefully gauge whether a complex or simple proposal is suitable. Proposals are vastly more likely to pass if informal consensus has been developed through negotiation, so it is unwise to blindly propose changes without checking to see if there is support elsewhere. You may waste everyone's time and may find yourself excluded from future negotiations! Second, once a motion is on the floor, informal negotiation and discussion stops. Third, regardless of the number of students in a delegation, each delegation has one vote. Fourth, proposals may change a limitless number of times; provided that the process above is followed, the Constitution may be amended from its original language, back to its original language, then in a new direction. There is certain to be some back-and-forth here. Finally, remember that if a change is approved, it is only a change to the proposed Constitution. Ratification is still necessary for the entire document to pass—and that requires positive votes from three-fourths of those present (ten of the thirteen states).

Keep in mind that if Congress is apportioned on the basis of equality rather than proportionality, slaves cannot be counted at all as people for the purposes of apportionment. When apportionment is established on the basis of equality, the answer to question 5 automatically becomes 'no.'

Moving to Ratify

At any time, you may move to ratify the document, as proposed in the Public Space. The motion to ratify must be seconded by a state, through the same procedure discussed above. At that point, all discussion stops and each state votes via roll-call, also as described above. If three-fourths of the delegations present (ten states in a thirteen-state game) vote for ratification, the game ends and scoring takes place. If this benchmark is not met, the game continues.

Scoring

Fundamentally, your goal is to 'win' by scoring more points than other states at the end of the game. The game ends under two conditions, described below.

Win Condition One: Ratification

First, if at any point three-fourths of all states vote to ratify the Constitution (as presented in the Public Space), the game ends and scores are immediately tallied. In a full Convention, this requires that ten states agree to the contents of the proposed Constitution. The actual vote can be called at any time by any state, but states are advised to consider pursuing the best deal possible, which often requires careful consideration and rejecting early proposals. If ratification does take place, each state's goals are revealed and their score tallied in the Public Space. Total points are calculated from the goals stated in your State Briefing. This calculation has two parts. First, points are earned for achieving primary goals—the key six salient issues stated at the outset of the game. Second, states may earn points for their Pet Projects, which are also listed on the State Briefing.

The total possible score for each state is 25 points—20 possible for fulfilling all primary goals, and 5 possible for fulfilling Pet Projects. Note, however, that due to the nature of overlapping and conflicting state interests, few, if any, will approach its hypothetical maximum.

To illustrate how scoring works, let us set aside Pet Projects and examine how the primary goals are scored (see Box 3.1 for an example).

Box 3.1 Sample Ratified Version of the Constitution

1. Should the states be bound in a permanent Union under a government that can wage war?

   • Yes.
   • 6 points if the Constitution is ratified, 0 points if it is not.

2. Should the national legislature have the power to tax?

   • Yes.
   • 4 points if the legislature has the authority to tax; 0 if points if the legislature does not have the authority to tax.

3. How should representation in that legislature be apportioned?

   • Representation should be apportioned on the basis of each state's population.
   • 3 points if seats in the legislature are apportioned on the basis of population; 0 points if seats are apportioned in equal numbers across states.

4. Should a chief executive exist and how should this executive be selected?

   • Yes, and they should be selected by the legislature.
   • 5 points if the chief executive is elected by the legislature; 0 points if the chief executive is not selected by the legislature.

5. Should slaves count as people for the purposes of apportionment?

   • Yes.
   • 2 points if slaves are counted as people for the purposes of apportionment; 0 points if slaves are not counted as people for the purposes of apportionment.

6. Should the importation of slaves be permitted?

- You have no position on this matter.

And the ratified version of the Constitution might look like this:

1. Should the states be bound in a permanent Union under a government that can wage war?

- Yes.

2. Should the national legislature have the power to tax?

- Yes.

3. How should representation in that legislature be apportioned?

- All states are given equal representation.

4. Should a chief executive exist and how should this executive be selected?

- The president is elected by the legislature.

5. Should slaves count as people for the purposes of apportionment?

- Yes.

6. Should the importation of slaves be permitted?

- No opinion.

The final score for this state would be:

> 6 (for creating a permanent Union) + 4 (for a legislature that may tax) + 0 (representation is not apportioned on the basis of population) + 5 (president elected by legislature) + 2 (slaves count as people for the purposes of apportionment) + 0 (no opinion on the importation of slaves) = 17 points.

Significantly, while the questions themselves cannot be changed, the Convention can propose any language that answers them. In other words, 'yes' and 'no' are not the only possible answers. Such creative proposals usually appear when coalitions of states compromise on an issue, or as part of a bargaining process. Some answers may provide fractional points in a way that you can easily calculate, as in the example below. Other answers may be very unusual or surprising. In these cases, ask your instructor, who can tell you how you might score in a given category if a proposal falls in one of these grey areas.

See Box 3.2 for an example of what the ratified version of the Constitution might be.

Box 3.2 Sample Ratified Version of the Constitution

1. Should the states be bound in a permanent Union under a government that can wage war?

   • Yes.

2. Should the national legislature have the power to tax?

   • Yes.

3. How should representation in that legislature be apportioned?

   • Two-thirds of seats in the national legislature will be apportioned on the basis of equality; one-third of seats will be apportioned on the basis of population.

4. Should a chief executive exist and how should this executive be selected?

   • The chief executive should be selected by random lottery.

5. Should slaves count as people for the purposes of apportionment?

   • Slaves should count as half a person for these purposes.

6. Should the importation of slaves be permitted?

   • No.

In this case, the scoring for the sample state would change:

   6 (for creating a permanent Union) + 4 (for a legislature that may tax) + 1 (one-third of seats are apportioned by population; state scores 1 point because one-third of seats are so apportioned) + 0 (a random lottery is not selection by legislature, so no points are scored) + .33 (slaves are regarded as half a person for the purposes of apportionment, so half of the possible 2 points awarded for

---

such apportionment are awarded; however, only one-third of the legislature is apportioned on the basis of population, and so only a third of this value is awarded) = 11.33 points.

Additionally, each state is given between one and three Pet Projects. These are essentially secret goals. Some are highly controversial and difficult to realize; others entail preventing other states from succeeding in their goals. Just as you should not share your primary goals with other groups, it is unwise to let others know what your Pet Projects are. If made part of the proposed Constitution (through the process described in the section below), they appear in the Public Space below or beside the six key questions. If part of the proposed Constitution, they are voted on along with ratification, and points earned are calculated when final scores are revealed. Examples of Pet Projects might include "earn 2 points if no additional provisions are introduced to the Constitution that protect the institution of slavery," "earn 3 points if slaves escaping into non-slave states must be returned to their states of origin," "earn 1 point if the chief executive is appointed for life," or "earn 2 points for each state, over the necessary 10, that vote to ratify the Constitution." As you can see, Pet Projects can often conflict with one another.

As you can see, Pet Projects can often conflict with one another (see Box 3.3).

Box 3.3 Example of a Set of Pet Projects

Earn 3 points if any additional provisions are inserted into the Constitution that protect the institution of slavery.

Earn 1 point if some additional provision is introduced that benefits small states.

Earn 1 point if no additional provisions are introduced that benefit large states.

And in the Public Space, beneath the six major questions of the Convention, the following language has been included:

The power of states to determine whether or not slavery is legal is forever reserved to those states.

> States shall receive a share of all tariffs arising from foreign trade on the basis of their population.
>
> You would earn 3 points for your Pet Projects from these two sentences. There is a clause that protects slavery (3 points), but there is no additional language in this example that supports the rights of small states. Also, because of the second sentence that splits tariff money according to population, there is indeed a provision that benefits large states, and so you would not earn points toward the third example Pet Project.

Win Condition Two: No Ratification

If states are unable to reach an agreement and ratify the Constitution by the time determined by the instructor, the game immediately ends. Your instructor will let you know when this time is. If this takes place, no Constitution was passed: the Articles of Confederation remain the document that governs relations between the thirteen former colonies.

In this case, scoring is very simple, because everything in the Public Space becomes irrelevant. States need only look at the first question on their informational sheets: should the states be bound in a permanent Union under a government that can wage war? As there was no agreement, the answer to this is 'no.' States receive points accordingly for this—and only this—category.

Some Final Strategic Considerations

The instructions above provide all the information that you need to simulate the Convention. However, there are some strategic considerations that you may wish to keep in mind.

1. First, please keep in mind that the game is *not* designed to simulate the actual compromises inherent to creating our Constitution. There are a wide variety of possible solutions, proposals, and paths to victory. Your goal is to maximize your delegation's points—if that means a patriotic embrace of the idea of national unity, so be it. But if it means being an obstructionist,

refusing to cooperate unless demands are met, or making your vote on ratification subject to demands, these may well be good strategies to pursue.

2. Even if you benefit from ratifying the Constitution, always remember that you want to maximize your overall point total relative to other players. Under some constellations of conditions, states score higher by *not* ratifying the Constitution than by ratifying a deal that scarcely benefits them. Remember, also, that because your objective is to score more points than other players, you will want to keep a close eye out for states that seem to be getting everything that they want.

3. It is probably not a good idea to accept the first few attempts at ratification unless you feel that you are in a very strong position. More generally, if you feel that you are behind, it is to your advantage to hold out on ratification, even if you ultimately intend to ratify. This will force states that are more eager to ratify to compromise with you.

4. Remember that each state has very different incentives. Some desperately want to sign the document at all costs; others do not want to sign it unless very specific conditions are made. Use this knowledge to your advantage, and try to figure out what other states want.

5. Please remember that if Congress is apportioned on the basis of equality rather than proportionality, slaves cannot be counted at all as people for the purposes of apportionment. If Congress is apportioned on the basis of equality, the answer to question 5 is set to 'no.'

6. Nobody is under any obligation to be honest in informal negotiations. Be aware that some states may attempt to create confusion or incite division between states.

Debriefing

Describing What Happened

1. What was your delegation's strategy for winning? How well did this strategy work?

2. Where any issues particularly difficult to resolve? How were they resolved?

3. There was a clear tension at the Convention between the desires of individual states and the needs of the country. Where did you see this? Provide details, such as specific names, events, and states.

4. When did you compromise, and why? What goals did you sacrifice and for what reason?

5. In your view, which state delegation performed best and why?

Relating the Game to the World

6. How did the document created by your class diverge from the historical Constitution?

7. How did the document created by your class conform to the historical Constitution?

8. How would your class's Constitution have affected the separation of powers and the power of the national government had it been implemented in the US?

9. Do you see any compromises that occurred during the game that might create conflict later in American history? If so, what were these, and how might they create conflict later on?

10. If the Constitution created by your class were still operational today, how do you think the American politics would be different?

Thinking Deeply

11. What does your time playing the game suggest to you about the experience of the historical framers of the Constitution? What challenges would they have faced that you did not?

12. What does your game experience say about the role and importance of compromise in politics, particularly regarding national constitutions?

13. If you knew at the start of the game what you know now, what would you say to the other delegations in order to make the Convention go more smoothly? What would you say to help make sure your state got what it wanted?

14. Do you believe that the creation of the Constitution was inevitable?

15. If you could encapsulate what you learned during this game into one sentence, what would that sentence be?

Creating New Ideas

16. Suppose that you are tasked with designing the details of the Constitution that your class has created.

    a. Do you add a Bill of Rights? Why or why not? If you do add one, what are three rights that it would include? If you do not add a Bill of Rights, identify three rights in the US's current Bill of Rights and explain why they are not needed.

    b. What powers should the legislature have under your class's Constitution?

    c. What do you include in the document to ensure that it will survive over two hundred years?

17. Create a survey and interview five friends outside of the class about their knowledge and attitudes toward the Constitution. What does this survey say about the level of political knowledge in this country?

18. Draft your own preamble to this Constitution. Be sure that it reflects the philosophical undercurrents of the Constitution that you created.

19. Write a speech in support of the proposed Constitution to explain why the people of the United States should adopt it.

20. Prepare five questions that you would ask the delegates to the Constitutional Convention if you had the ability to interview them.

4

Hard-Won Equality

A Game About Social Movements

Overview

The Civil Rights Movement, the Women's Rights Movement, Abolitionism, and the LGBTQIA+ Rights Movement are all examples of large networks of people working to change an aspect of American society. Each of these networks has worked in an informal collaboration of individuals and groups, and they often operated outside of formal government institutions. In the social sciences, we give these networks a specific label: social movements. Social movements are challenging to define because no two are exactly alike. The issues they champion, the populations they represent, the people who participate in them, the methods they use, and the resistance they face can all vary greatly from movement to movement. They are simultaneously non-hierarchical and also surprisingly coordinated. They may exist only to serve one goal or may persist for decades, continually pushing for greater and greater advances. What social movements have in common, though, is that they all seek a societal change that is important to them, but which is not being accomplished through politics as usual. So, they take to the streets. They march, write letters, recruit supporters, hold sit-ins, rally, share information, fund-raise, and attract media attention. They may also go on hunger strikes, confront authority figures, register voters, challenge preconceptions and assumptions, hold vigils, and stop work. Their tactics are so varied that it would be impossible for one game to capture them all. The game you are about to play aims instead to emulate the struggles that social movements face in trying to coordinate their actions and achieve goals despite the diversity of voices they contain.

In this game, you will play in a group representing a social movement organization (SMO). SMOs are well-defined groups within social movements that provide leadership and organization to the movement. For example, there were many key SMOs in the Civil Rights Movement, such as the National Association for the Advancement of Colored People (NAACP), the Student Nonviolent Coordinating Committee (SNCC), and the Congress of Racial Equality (CORE). Each of these groups helped to shape and guide the broader movement. Yet, they also had their own priorities and perspectives. For example, the SNCC was much more willing than other SMOs to engage in direct action in opposition-heavy states like Mississippi. Because SMOs each have their own preferences for the future of the movement, their interactions can be a mix of cooperation and competition. The game reflects this by having each SMO strive to have the most of one kind of score (Prestige) while also working with other groups to build a shared score for the whole movement (Equality).

The set of four SMOs in this game does not represent any particular social movement. Rather, each SMO in the game resembles a common kind of real-world SMO. There are the Students, who are energetic and bold but lack the resources of more established groups. The Moderates have great reach and appeal but are not willing to upset the status quo. Religious Organizations can lay claim to moral authority and utilize their existing institutional network for coordinating protest actions. Radicals are not content with conventional tactics and seek to challenge society through confrontation. Each of these groups will have different actions they can take in the game reflecting their distinct natures. Each group can win, but which one will? Will your SMO be able to further the goals of the social movement and achieve greatness for itself? We wish you luck in this game, which pushes you to both cooperate and compete in order to win.

Instructions and Rules

Goals: Equality and Prestige

Players are grouped into four SMOs: Students, Moderates, Religious Organizations, and Radicals. Each SMO in the game has two goals. First, an SMO must help the broader social movement achieve greater legal and cultural equality. This is measured by the Equality score, to which all groups contribute and which starts at 0. If Equality does not reach 4.5 by the end of the game, the movement has failed, and all SMOs lose the game. There are three ways to gain Equality throughout the game: petitioning the courts, passing bills through Congress, and achieving acceptance in culture.

Second, each SMO desires prominence and influence within the larger movement. This is measured by the Prestige score. Unlike Equality, each SMO has its own Prestige score, and the SMO with the highest Prestige at the end of the game wins. Prestige is acquired when your SMO successfully increases the movement's Equality score. Remember, if Equality does not exceed 4.5 at the end of the game, nobody wins, and so Prestige becomes irrelevant. Whoever has the highest Prestige in a successful game is crowned the Leader of the Movement and is the winner.

Gameplay

Your group can increase Prestige and Equality scores by performing actions. Actions in this game come in several types. Some actions spend resources to try to increase Prestige and Equality. Others generate resources, increase the likelihood of increasing Prestige and Equality, or perform a function unique to an SMO. Your group can take any action available to it as many times and in whatever order you wish, providing that (1) your group is able to pay any costs associated with the action, and (2) your group has not exceeded its maximum number of actions. For most groups this maximum number is ten, and for the Students SMO it is fifteen. Because of this crucial limit, it is important to carefully strategize with your groupmates about the best combination of ten (or fifteen) actions to take in order to maximize the Prestige that your group accumulates.

The set of actions available to your SMO reflects the nature of your SMO. For example, the Students SMO has fewer options than other groups, symbolizing how students have less access to resources than more established elements of society. However, Students can also perform more actions over the course of the game, which represents their youthful energy and flexible schedules. Like the Students, each group in the game will have its own strengths and weaknesses deriving from the actions it can perform. Each group should still have a roughly equal chance of winning the game, though, and so what matters most is how well your group uses the actions available to it and how well you consider the possible actions of others.

Your SMO will also have the option to work together with other SMOs in Joint Actions. With a Joint Action, two or more SMOs perform the same action at the same time. Each of the SMOs participating in the Joint Action use up one of their available actions, but they also all benefit from working together. The costs of the action may be reduced, or the benefits may be increased compared to performing the action alone. It is also true that not all groups can perform all actions, so Joint Actions are a way for some groups to benefit from the options available to others. Generally speaking, it is always more efficient to perform a Joint Action than a solo action. Importantly, the group with access to the action being used in the Joint Action controls who can join and who is excluded.

Procedure for Taking Actions

Any SMO may take an action at any time. To take an action, a group representative raises a hand and is recognized by the instructor. At that point, the representative moves to a place designated by the instructor, which is called 'taking the Spotlight.' The Spotlight represents the media and public attention that come with taking an important action. This SMO representative may only take one action when taking the Spotlight and, when completed with that action, must return to their seat before raising their hand again. Other SMOs who wish to be recognized may have raised their hand during, after, or before the action and may keep their hands raised as long as they wish. In the event that multiple SMOs raise their hands at once, the instructor will select the SMO whose member has had their hand raised longest. An SMO may take the Spotlight several times in a row, but only if nobody else has raised their hand. If this is difficult to determine, the instructor will make a judgment at his or her discretion.

Types of SMOs

Four SMOs are represented in this game. Each comprises an important element of this hypothetical social movement. Each group is able to take a slightly different set of actions. All SMOs have a store of Resources, which represent an amalgam of money, influence, organization, and people power. All SMOs have the ability to increase their Resources. Resources are spent to increase Tolerance in Congress and Culture, or to take actions that attempt to increase Equality. These SMOs are listed below.

1. Students are a young and restive segment of the population whose energy is important for pressing for change. They start the game with no Resources because they are not as established in life as other groups. However, their flexible schedules are also an advantage in that they can use more actions over the course of the game—fifteen in total.

2. Moderates are large in number and are distributed across society. This gives them a diverse set of tools for scoring points. However, they are also more reluctant to push for dramatic change than other groups, and their possible actions reflect this. Moderates start with two Resources.

3. Religious Organizations are well organized, well funded, and have access to people in power. They can also use their existing infrastructure (religious buildings and social groups) to help organize movement actions. Religious Organizations start with four Resources.

4. Radicals are the angry, the discontented, and the marginalized. Radicals desire change through any means possible and want it now. Radicals start the game with no Resources.

Types of Actions

The actions that SMOs may take are divided into four categories: Resource-Generating Actions, Scoring Actions, Tolerance-
Increasing Actions, and SMO-Specific Actions.

Resource-Generating Actions

All groups have access to an action that increases their Resources
by two. Other actions use Resources, and so generating enough
to meet your needs is important. All of these actions function the
same way. They are:

Hold a Sit-In

Available to Students. Students hold a national, organized,
and peaceful protest where they occupy some location and
refuse to move.

Hold Peaceful Rallies

Available to Moderates. Moderates organize rallies across the
country to build political support and raise money.

Fund-Raising Campaign

Available to Religious Organizations. Using their immense
mailing lists and many pulpits, Religious Organizations
executes a fund-raising movement to raise money for the
movement.

Disruptive Protests

Available to Radicals. Taking to the streets with signs, shouting,
and demonstrations, Radicals increase their visibility and
incorporate new members into their folds.

Scoring Actions

All groups can perform at least one action that attempts to increase
the movement's Equality score and their own Prestige score. Each
of these actions costs four Resources. Upon paying the Resources,
the group rolls a die. If the roll is successful, Prestige and Equality increase. A successful roll must be lower than the Tolerance of
Change of the institution they are attempting to influence. Three
such institutions are available for influence: Congress, Culture, or

the Courts. Tolerance of Change represents the fact that different parts of society can be more or less resistant to change. For example, a conservative Court may be intolerant to change, or a particular Congress may feel that change is a good thing. Tolerance varies from 0 to 6.

Scoring actions are:

Change Culture

Available to Moderates, Students, and Radicals. Through initiating dialogue with communities across campuses nationwide, the SMO attempts to increase Equality. For the cost of four Resources, the SMO can roll a die. If the die roll is *beneath* culture's Tolerance of Change, the SMO gains 1 Prestige, culture's Tolerance of Change is reduced by 2, and Equality increases by 1 (note: if Culture's Perception of the Movement has successfully been changed once previously, Equality increases by .5; if it has been changed twice, Equality increases by .25 for each further successful increase).

Write a Bill

Available to Moderates and Religious Organizations. By using their political clout, an SMO pressures Congressional representatives to write a bill demanding more political equality. For the cost of four Resources, the SMO can roll a die. If the die roll is *beneath* Congress's Tolerance of Change, the SMO gains 1 Prestige, Congress's Tolerance of Change is reduced by 2, and Equality increases by 1 (note: if writing a bill has at any point successfully increased Equality, a successful roll increases Equality by .5; if writing a bill has successfully increased Equality more than twice, a successful role increases Equality by .25 for each further successful increase).

Litigate

Available to Moderates and Religious Organizations. By utilizing their legal resources, the SMO works to change policy through the judicial system. For the cost of four Resources, the SMO can roll a die. If the die roll is *beneath* the Courts' Tolerance of Change, the SMO gains 1 Prestige, and equality increases by one (note: if Congress's Perception of the Movement has successfully been changed once previously,

Equality increases by .5; if it has been changed twice, Equality increases by .25). This action can only take place successfully once for each composition of the Court, which changes every twenty minutes.

The example in Box 4.1 illustrates how these actions influence gameplay.

Box 4.1 Gameplay Example

Congress's Tolerance for Change is 3. The Moderates decide to take a gamble and attempt to increase Equality through using the 'Write a Bill' option. They raise their hand and are recognized by the instructor, then take the Spotlight and roll a die. Because it is a 2, which is beneath Congress's Tolerance for Change, they are successful. They gain 1 Prestige and Congress's Tolerance for Change decreases to 1. However, because Equality has already been increased through Congress once, only .5 Equality is gained for the movement.

Tolerance-Increasing Actions

You can increase the odds of your scoring actions succeeding by increasing the Tolerance of Change held by Congress or Culture. The Court's Tolerance of Change cannot be affected by SMOs, and is determined by a die roll by the instructor conducted every twenty minutes. Each action of this type costs two Resources and increases Tolerance of a given institution by 1. Tolerances can be increased to a maximum of 6.

Tolerance-increasing actions are:

Lobby Congress
Available to Moderates and Religious Organizations. For the cost of two Resources, increase Congress's Tolerance of Change by 1.

Inspire Popular Culture
Available to Students, Moderates, and Radicals. For the cost of two Resources, increase Culture's Tolerance of Change by 1.

SMO-Specific Actions

Two SMOs—Radicals and Religious Organizations—each have unique actions that only they can take. These are defined below. The other two SMOs enjoy different advantages—Students can take fifteen actions instead of ten, and Moderates have access to all three of the different scoring actions.

The two SMO-specific actions are:

God's Glory

Available to Religious Organizations. Religious Organizations have natural followers throughout key positions in the media, government, and other important sectors of society. For an action, Religious Organizations can increase their Prestige by .25.

Violent Infiltration

Available to Radicals. Frustrated that their demands are not being met, Radicals infiltrate an event held by another SMO and initiate violent protest. As a result, leaders and the general public often misattribute the origins of Radical-led violence and wrongly conclude that other groups may be responsible. For an action, Radicals Steal .25 Prestige from another group and appropriate it for themselves.

For your convenience, each SMO and its available actions are sketched in Table 4.1.

TABLE 4.1 SMO Actions

	Resource Generating Actions	Scoring Actions			Tolerance-Increasing Actions		SMO-specific Actions	
	Generate Resources	Change Culture	Write a Bill	Litigate	Lobby Congress	Inspire Popular Culture	God's Glory	Violent Infiltration
Students	X	X					X	
Moderates	X	X	X	X	X	X		
Religious Orgs	X		X	X	X		X	
Radicals	X	X				X		X

Joint Actions

Two or more SMOs may perform an action together. Such Joint Actions are more efficient than acting alone but may not always be the right choice for your group. To initiate a Joint Action, the SMO initiating the action as well as supporting SMOs must all raise their hands to be recognized. The SMO with the action states that they are conducting a Joint Action and gets to decide who can and cannot participate in the Joint Action. No SMO can join if uninvited, and invited SMOs are not obligated to join in that action. It's always a good idea to decide which SMOs will participate in a Joint Action, and who will initiate it, before attempting to take the Spotlight, otherwise you will waste quite a lot of time. All SMOs joining in the Joint Action send a representative to the Spotlight together. Any such group is part of the action and so should not have any members with raised hands where the group is gathered (in other words, those SMOs not participating in a Joint Action will take actions before any SMO engaged in the action, provided that these non-participating SMOs have raised their hands).

The participating SMOs each spend one of their total actions, but they gain benefits from working together. All SMOs involved in a Joint Action must spend an action, and all must send one (and only one) representative to the Spotlight.

- For Resource-Generating Actions (Hold a Sit-In, Hold Peaceful Rallies, Fund-Raising Campaigns, and Protests), the SMOs involved gain two Resources plus the number of participating SMOs.
- For Tolerance-Increasing Actions (Inspire Popular Culture or Lobbying Congress), the increase in Tolerance becomes the total number of SMOs participating in the action. All participating SMOs must spend two Resources when contributing to this action.
- For Scoring Actions (Writing a Bill, Changing Culture, Litigating), the likelihood of success increases because each SMO obtains a die, and the Equality increases if *any* SMO succeeds in their role. All participating SMOs gain the usual amount of Prestige. All participating SMOs must spend four Resources as usual.
- SMO-Specific Actions cannot be performed as Joint Actions.

Box 4.2 illustrates how this works.

Box 4.2 Gameplay Example

The Moderates, Students, and Religious Organizations agree to jointly Hold a Sit-In. The Radicals want to join in, but because Sit-Ins can only be initiated by Students, it's up to the Students to decide if the Radicals can participate. Because the Radicals have been Stealing everyone's Prestige, the Students opt to proceed with just the Moderates and Religious Organizations. A representative from each group raises their hand and the instructor directs them to the Spotlight. They take the Joint Action. All three groups gain five Resources (2 + 1 for each SMO participating). All three groups spend one action. The Radicals, who raised their hands as soon as the other SMOs approached the Spotlight, are then called to the Spotlight. In revenge for being excluded, they conduct a Violent Infiltration of the Students, Stealing .25 of their Prestige.

The current Court's Tolerance for Change is 3, and nobody has used the Court to increase Equality in this twenty-minute cycle (remember, the Court's Tolerance for Change is randomly determined every twenty minutes, but the Courts can only be used to successfully increase Equality each twenty minutes). The Moderates know it's a bad gamble, so they initiate a Joint Action with the Students to Litigate. A member of each group raises their hand and the instructor recognizes them. They take the Spotlight. Each pays an action and four Resources. The Moderates roll a 3, which does not increase Equality because it is not below the Court's Tolerance for Change. The Students roll a 4, which does not increase Equality. Both return to their seats, dejected.

The Public Space

The Public Space for this game will look something like Table 4.2.

Scoring

The instructor will update the Public Space as groups take their actions. The game ends if all teams have used up their actions or if the time designated to play the game elapses. If the class has failed to reach the required Equality threshold, everybody loses. If the Equality threshold has been met or surpassed, the SMO with the highest Prestige is the victor.

TABLE 4.2 Public Space for Hard-Won Equality

SMO Information			
SMO	Resources	Remaining Actions	Prestige
Students	0	15	0
Moderates	2	10	0
Religious Organizations	4	10	0
Radicals	0	10	0

Equality: 0

Scoring Information			
Institution	Tolerance of Change	# Successful Attempts to Change Equality	Increase in Equality on Next Successful Attempt
Courts	*	0	1
Congress	2	0	1
Culture	2	0	1

Debriefing

Describing What Happened

1. Did any group appear to have a natural advantage over other groups in this game? Why or why not?
2. When did cooperation occur in the game?
3. Do you think that the game could be won without any level of cooperation? Why or why not?
4. What was the single most decisive moment in the game?
5. Why do you think that the winner of the game won?

Relating the Game to the World

6. Think about a contemporary social movement, and name an important SMO within that social movement. What SMO in the game is most similar to the SMO you have chosen? Identify two similarities.

7. Using the SMO that you identified in the previous question, determine if that SMO uses any of the tactics available to SMOs in this game.

8. Identify one example of a big social change that arose primarily due to high levels of public pressure. Identify one example of a big social change that happened largely because of government taking action, perhaps even before public opinion supported it.

9. The tactics that social movements use change with the times. What is one way that a social movement has adopted a new technology or media to pursue its goals?

10. Whether or not you are a member of a SMO, what is one way that you can help a group move toward the acquisition of greater equality in the United States?

Thinking Deeply

11. One goal in this game is to be crowned Leader of the Movement. What is one example of a SMO that became Leader of a Movement in real life? You may need to conduct some research to answer this question.

12. How could you change the rules of the game to make achieving Equality easier? Describe what this change would look like in the real world.

13. In the real world, do social movements ever end? Is there a hypothetical ceiling of equality where social movements are satisfied and cease pushing for equality? Or is the quest for greater equality a never-ending struggle? Support your answer with examples.

14. Based on what you observed in the game, what are some of the primary obstacles to the success of social movements? Can these obstacles be circumvented? If so, how?

15. Describe one social movement that is currently underway in this country. Evaluate its successes and failures.

Creating New Ideas

16. What is a type of SMO that is not present in the game but is present in the real world? How would you represent it in this game (what abilities would you assign it)?

17. Select a social issue that is important to you. Describe a new SMO that might emerge during a struggle to advance this cause. What strategies might this SMO use?

18. The social movement is over; it has succeeded. Write a newspaper column denouncing or affirming the actions of the Radicals.

19. In this game, Students use Sit-Ins to generate attention, but in the real world, student groups use other tactics as well. What tactics would students at your campus utilize in their quest for social change?

20. Aside from occasional radical violence, this game offers a largely civil perspective on social change. But there have been times in human history where bullets, rather than ballots, have determined outcomes. Should violence ever be used in the pursuit of rights? What limitations, if any, should be placed on such actions?

Nomination Scrimmage

A Game About Primary/ Caucus Strategy

Overview

It has already been a long campaign for the Republican nomination for the presidency. First, Iowa was a draw for most candidates, and New Hampshire failed to produce a solid front-runner. Nevada and South Carolina failed to clarify the picture, although some minor candidates have dropped off, leaving only five viable candidates. The time for a decisive contest is at hand.

So, it is time to gear up for Super Tuesday! On March 1, twelve contests will be held across the United States, which will certainly mark a turning point in the fortunes of the presidential contenders. This promises to be a decisive moment in the campaign. It's up to you to help win it.

You and your group will serve as senior campaign strategists for one of five candidates who want one thing: to earn the most delegates to the Republican National Convention and help secure your candidate's nomination to the presidency. Your candidates are, at this point, blank slates: they are not based on any historical personality. Their ideology and issue positions are yours to shape. In doing so, you will carefully study the field, determine how you want your candidate to appeal to the world, and decide where you want to flex your resources. The strategic considerations are many, and competition is fierce. Who will emerge the victor?

Instructions and Rules

Gameplay

In this game, your group will develop issue positions for an imagined candidate and calculate how liberal or conservative these choices make the candidate. This value, as well as the issue positions that you adopt, will affect how expensive it is to campaign in different states. All candidates, drawing from a finite pool of resources, will then make investments of time and energy in different states (called Placements). You will thus be forced to consider an initial strategy: is your goal to stack all of your resources in a few high-value, winner-take-all states where you can compete easily? Would you rather have modest appeal to a wider range of states, enabling you to play off of competitors' actions? Do you want to move to the far-left or far-right wings of the party or plant yourself in the center?

The game is intended to offer some insight into the decisions made by candidates and their staff during the primary season, but it contains some important abridgements and deviations from reality that were necessary to ensure smooth gameplay. The goal of this game is not to simulate the 2016 Super Tuesday contest verbatim (or any other past or future primary), but rather to allow players to delve into the strategic mechanisms that populate the caucus and primary season. The ideological dispositions and important issues of each state are approximations based on the exit polls of the 2016 Presidential Super Tuesday returns but are not intended to absolutely reflect reality. For simplicity's sake, delegates are awarded based on winner-take-all and proportional rules; this knowingly sidesteps the question of superdelegates, Pledged Delegates, and other, more complex ways that delegates are awarded on Super Tuesday. The concept of thresholds—that candidates must win a certain percentage of the state's total vote share to earn delegates—is ignored, largely due to the varying ways that states handle this remainder. This game assumes that all candidates enter

Super Tuesday on equal footing, which is seldom the case, and the viable field of five candidates is somewhat large compared to the historical norm for this point in the campaign. Delegate totals and apportionment rules may well change following publication of this game, and so should be viewed as abstractions used to understand campaign dynamics rather than facts to memorize. In some cases, to provide good opportunities for different types of strategies that would typically take place over a longer campaign, we mix winner-take-all (WTA) and proportional rules for the allocation of delegates, even though all states in the 2016 Super Tuesday contest used proportional rules or some hybridized version of WTA and proportionality. The issues important to the caucus and primary-going members of each electorate are somewhat arbitrarily assigned. Finally, the selection of Republican primaries and caucuses is not meant to emphasize Republican politics; in selecting which party to feature, we simply flipped a coin.

Sequence of Play

Setup

Students (as groups) take the role of campaign advisors for one of five candidates for president during Super Tuesday. The candidates are Alan Abernathy, Bob Ball, Carrie Crohn, Duke Van Dyke, and Emily Emi. Before the game begins, groups will be provided with a Candidate Profile for the candidate. On this sheet, you will decide what your candidate's positions on issues will be and then calculate the extent to which these positions align with the collective desires of primary or caucus voters in each state. The positions that you select cannot change throughout the course of the game. A sample Candidate Profile is listed below in Tables 5.1, 5.2, and 5.3.

Your first task will be to calculate your Candidate Ideology, which represents how liberal or conservative you are. The lower the number, the more liberal your candidate is. Before selecting your positions on issues, though, you should consider the 'State Information' section of your Candidate Profile found in Table 5.3. This table lists a few important things to think about before making any irreversible choices. First, it lists two issue positions that are especially important to the primary or caucus-going voters of each state. Next, it lists the

TABLE 5.1 Ideological Dispositions

	Moderate (0)	Middle-Right (1)	Far-Right (2)
Abortion	Abortion should be legal only in cases of rape and incest.	All abortions should be illegal.	All abortions should be illegal and past abortions should be prosecuted as murder.
Defense	Defense spending should remain at current levels.	Defense spending should increase by a small percentage.	Defense spending should increase by a large percentage.
Gun Control	Only minimal restrictions should be added to existing gun laws.	Gun laws should stay as they are.	Restrictions on gun ownership should be loosened.
Government Size	The government should not increase spending and should reduce taxes.	The government should reduce spending and taxes.	The government should make massive cuts to spending, taxes, and its role in American society.
Immigration	Immigration laws should be reformed.	Immigration should be restricted.	Immigration should be greatly restricted.

TABLE 5.2 Key Positions

Abortion	Abortion should be illegal.	Infrastructure	Infrastructure should be a priority.
Education	School vouchers are good policy.	Marijuana	States should decide marijuana policy.
Energy	Clean energy is a good investment.	Parks	Federal lands should be given to states.
Environment	Conservatism includes conservation.	Prisons	Prisons should be privatized.
Health Care	Entitlements should be cut.	States' Rights	States know what is best for themselves.
Immigration	Immigration should be restricted.	Taxes	Taxes should be reduced.

TABLE 5.3 State Information

State	KP #1	KP #2	Ideology	Delegates	Type	CS
Alabama	Abortion	Immigration	8	50	WTA	
Alaska	States Rights	Marijuana	1	28	P	
Arkansas	Education	Taxes	3	40	WTA	
Colorado	Marijuana	States Rights	5	37	WTA	
Georgia	Taxes	Prisons	2	76	P	
Massachusetts	Immigrations	Prisons	4	42	P	
Minnesota	Infrastructure	Parks	3	38	WTA	
Oklahoma	Prisons	Energy	10	43	WTA	
Tennessee	Parks	Health Care	8	58	WTA	
Texas	Energy	Abortion	8	155	P	
Vermont	Environment	Parks	3	16	WTA	

aggregated Ideology of the state's electorate. The following two columns describe the total number of delegates available in the primary or caucus, and the type of contest that it is. There are two types: winner-take-all (WTA) or proportional (P). In a winner-take-all contest, whichever candidate has the highest vote share wins all of the delegates at the end of the game. In a proportional contest, candidates receive delegates proportional to the amount of support that they earn. Earning vote share is described later in these instructions.

After you have studied the state information in Table 5.3 carefully, it is time to fill out the Candidate Profile as a group. The instructor will determine how much time is allowed to complete this task. Before doing so, however, you will certainly want to read the rest of these instructions to understand the importance of your actions and how the game is played and won (or lost). Remember: once you have filled out your Candidate Profile, there is no turning back.

To fill out your Profile, follow these steps:

1. Circle a position in each row under the 'Ideological Dispositions' columns in Table 5.1. You will do so by selecting the moderate, middle-right, or far-right position on each of five issues: abortion, defense spending, gun control, government size, and immigration. After selecting one position per row, you will tally

your candidate's Ideology score. This score will range from 0 to 10 and will represent how moderate or extreme your candidate's conservatism is. Give your candidate a 0 for each position in the 'Moderate' column, a 1 for each position in the 'Middle-Right' column, and a 2 for each position in the 'Far-Right' column. Sum these numbers together for your candidate's total Ideology score.

2. Next, you will select two Key Positions for your candidate by circling them in Table 5.2. These are issue positions that your candidate has taken special care to incorporate into their messaging, advertisements, and branding. Key Positions will provide an advantage in states where these issues are important.

3. Calculate your Congruence Score for each state in two steps. First, compute the general ideological distance between the candidate and the state's primary/caucus-goers by subtracting your Ideology from each state's Ideology score. If you end up with a negative number from this, make it positive (in mathematical terms, take the absolute value). Next, subtract 1 if the state has one of your candidate's policy interests as one of its Key Issues; subtract 2 if the state has both of your candidate's policy interests as its Key Issues. Performing these operations for each state will leave you with different Congruence Scores for each state. However, your score cannot be lower than 1 for any state, so if any of your Congruence Scores are 0 or below, raise them to 1. When complete, record the Congruence Score for each state in the Congruence Score column in Table 5.3.

To illustrate, consider the example in Box 5.1.

Box 5.1 Gameplay Example

Alan Abernathy has an Ideology of 5. The Ideology of Alabama's primary/caucus-goers is 8. To determine his Congruence Score with Alabama, Alan first subtracts 5 from 8, leaving him with -3. Because this number cannot be negative, it becomes a positive 3. He shares no Key Issues with the state, and so 3 is his final Congruence Score. In mathematical terms, the calculation is $|5-8|-0$.

Next, Alan Abernathy calculates his Congruence Score with Alaska. Again, his Ideology is 5, and the Ideology of Alaska's Republicans is 1. However, Alan has designated marijuana decriminalization as one of this Key Issues, which is shared with Alaska. So, Alan first subtracts 1 from 5, leaving him with 4. Then, he subtracts 1 because he shares a Key Position with Alaska. In mathematical terms, the calculation is $|5 - 1| - 1 = 3$ Alan records 3 for his Congruence Score.

Once you have calculated a Congruence Score for each state, you are finished with the setup for the game. Double check your calculations and await the instructor's indication for the game to begin.

Rounds

Each player starts the game with thirty resources. Resources represent an amalgam of time, energy, money, campaign staff, air time, interviews, and other things that candidates use to win elections. In each round, candidates will make up to three 'Placements.' Each Placement represents an allocation of resources given to a state and costs as many resources as the Congruence Score for that state. Play begins with Mr. Abernathy and proceeds alphabetically; when Mrs. Emi has completed her Placements, play returns to Mr. Abernathy.

Placements and the related expenditure of resources are represented in the Public Space, as shown below. On a candidate's turn, the spokesperson will announce their Placements and the cost of each Placement (again, the Congruence Score for that state). The instructor will then update the Public Space to reflect these Placements and the change in resources. If a candidate is caught misrepresenting the cost of a Placement, their candidate loses ten resources. Each candidate has a time determined by the instructor to make their Placements and so groups are advised to think ahead. If this time elapses and no Placements are made, that group is penalized by one resource and play passes to the next player.

The game continues until a certain amount of time (determined by the instructor) has elapsed or when candidates no longer have enough resources to make Placements. If at any time a candidate cannot continue to make a Placement, but others can, that candidate will no longer be able to participate. So, it is wise to think carefully and strategically and pay attention to others. Candidates may not pass their turn and must always make at least one Placement (or be penalized by one resource). However, candidates may find that they have unused resources should the game end due to its time limit elapsing. In this case, remaining resources are simply wasted.

The Public Space

The Public Space for this game will look something like Table 5.4.

Scoring

When the game ends, the instructor tabulates the score. For winner-take-all primaries or caucuses, whoever has the most Placements in the state takes all of the delegates. In the event of a tie, a coin flip determines the winner. For proportional primaries or caucuses, candidates are awarded a proportion of delegates equal to their

TABLE 5.4 Resource Placements

State	Delegates	Type	Abernathy	Ball	Crohn	Van Dyke	Emi	Candidate Resources	
Alabama	50	WTA	4	0	0	3	0	Abernathy:	20
Alaska	28	P	2	2	2	0	0	Ball:	26
Arkansas	40	WTA	0	0	0	0	5	Crohn:	28
Colorado	37	WTA	0	0	0	0	0	Van Dyke:	25
Georgia	76	P	0	0	0	0	0	Emi:	25
Massachusetts	42	P	0	0	0	0	0		
Minnesota	38	WTA	0	0	0	0	0		
Oklahoma	43	WTA	0	0	0	0	0		
Tennessee	58	WTA	0	0	0	0	0		
Texas	155	P	0	0	0	0	0		
Vermont	16	WTA	0	0	0	0	0		

placement. If you are due to receive a fraction of a delegate in a state, your final delegate count for that state is rounded to the nearest whole number.

Debriefing

Describing What Happened

1. What was your strategy in building out your Candidate Profile? Was it successful?

2. What was your strategy for making Placements? Did you target certain states? How did you react to the moves of your opponents?

3. Did anyone in your class 'run from the left' and try to run as a moderate Republican? How did they perform? If not, why do you think no one chose this approach?

4. Were there any opportunities or reasons for candidates to cooperate or collude at any point in the game? Where it did not occur, what were the barriers to this cooperation?

5. Did you or your group make any important miscalculations or mistakes during the game? What were these?

Relating the Game to the World

6. This game assumes that all candidates enter Super Tuesday with the same number of Resources, but this is almost never true in actual campaigns. What things might help a candidate with less funding and resources win a primary election?

7. Resources are prominently used in this game. What are some of the many things that Resources represent?

8. Placements are another important concept in the game. What do Placements represent in the real world?

9. Real-world primaries and caucuses make use of 'thresholds,' or a minimum percentage of the vote required to receive any delegates in a proportionally allocated contest. How do you think that the game would change if, say, a 20% threshold were enacted?

10. Candidates expend their campaign resources in a variety of ways beyond campaign stops or 'Placements,' as this game calls them. What are some things that a candidate might do to woo voters in Alaska, Massachusetts, and Colorado that are not campaign stops? Provide at least one different answer for each state that suits that state's interests.

Thinking Deeply

11. To what extent do you think this is a realistic simulation of Super Tuesday? Where does it emulate reality, and where does it deviate from it? Feel free to use information contained in the game itself to help answer this question.

12. Based on your experience with this game, which candidates do you feel would have the ability to continue on into the next primaries? Which one has the best chance at winning a general election against a generic Democrat? Explain your answers.

13. This game simulates two ways of apportioning delegates to candidates: through winner-take-all and proportionality. Which do you think is the fairest, and why?

14. Super Tuesday has a decidedly southern geographical focus, with most of the delegates being drawn from Southern states. Because Super Tuesday is often the decisive contest, do you think that this geographical concentration in one region is good or bad for selecting the most competitive candidate? Why or why not?

15. All in all, is Super Tuesday a fair way to contribute to the selection of a Party's nominee for president? Why or why not?

Creating New Ideas

16. Presidential primary seasons are long and give a lot of influence to states early in the process (like Iowa and New Hampshire). Design a new primary system for the Republican Party that would treat states more equally and make the whole process shorter. Explain how this system would work and why it would or would not be better than the current system.

17. Create a diary entry for your candidate, written as if your candidate was experiencing the game's events as if they were playing out in an actual Super Tuesday. Have the diary entry explain your candidate's personal fears and goals for Super Tuesday as well as your candidate's thoughts about the outcome.

18. The Candidate Profiles for this game were created with categories and Key Issues that would typically appeal to most Republicans because this game focuses on a Republican Super Tuesday. But what if this were a Democratic contest? Design a Candidate Profile (with new Ideological Dispositions and Key Positions) for a Democratic candidate competing in the Democratic Super Tuesday.

19. Prepare a campaign advertisement for the winner of the contest. This should take the form of a description of a brief thirty-second video slot explaining the candidate's qualifications and positions.

20. Prepare an attack ad aimed at the winner of the contest. This should take the form of a description of a brief thirty-second video slot thrashing the candidate.

6

Written by Committee

A Game About Lawmaking

Overview

Making a federal law in the United States is a convoluted process. A bill will wind its way through negotiation, committees, amendments, and votes in two houses of Congress before reaching the president's desk to be signed. The game you are about to play will focus on a specific part of this process. You will be a member of Congress attending a conference committee. These committees form when the House of Representatives and the Senate cannot agree on what the final bill sent on to the president should look like. They each send some of their members to resolve their differences in a temporary committee formed just for that purpose, called a conference committee. The negotiations that take place in the committee are guided by many of the same factors that shape the larger lawmaking process: constituent expectations, partisan rivalry, interest group pressures, legislators' personal beliefs and goals, media attention, and the vagaries of the current political climate, among other things. This makes conference committees something of a microcosm for lawmaking as a whole and consequently an excellent setting for a game on lawmaking. In this game, you will work with the other players to find a compromise that can pass out of the committee but which also meets your own legislator's interests. Balancing what you hope to achieve with what is actually possible will be challenging, but that is the art of politics. We wish you luck.

Instructions and Rules

Gameplay

How will negotiations in the game work? They will be freeform in the sense that you and the other players serving on this committee will be able to mingle, plan, ponder, bribe, refuse, conspire, grandstand, hedge, and implore as much as you want. Your shared goal will be for a majority of Senators and a majority of Representatives on the committee to find common ground on three policy disagreements. Each of these disagreements comes from a difference between House and Senate versions of a massive federal lands bill, and these differences must be fixed before the bill can move forward. The first area of disagreement relates to something the Democrats want. Because the Senate is controlled by Democrats, the Senate version of the bill calls for the creation of a trust fund for maintaining federal lands that is not included in the House bill. The fund's money, if later set aside by Congress in an appropriations bill, would go toward repairing park infrastructure, protecting wildlife, and preserving forests. Your committee has to work out just how expansive this fund's operations should be as measured in funding.

Table 6.1 portrays the range of possible positions a legislator can take on the issue of the trust fund. If a legislator has position 0, it means that they want no federal dollars to be given to the fund. This would be a more conservative position because conservatives believe in limiting both federal spending and the size of the federal

TABLE 6.1 Issue Area One

Issue One—American Parks Trust Fund

0	1	2	3	4	5	6	7	8	9
$0 for fund			$1 billion for fund			$2 billion for fund			$3 billion for fund

government. Consequently, you will see a lot of Republican legislators in the game preferring that the final bill take a position somewhere around 0 on the issue of the trust fund. Democrats will typically want substantial amounts of money for the fund and will have their preferences somewhere around 6 on the scale (or $2 billion). The example legislator in Table 6.1 has a preference of 4, indicated by the gray shading, meaning that she wants about $1.33 billion to be allocated to the fund. The legislator that you will be playing will have his or her own preference given on a Preference Sheet distributed to you by your instructor. You will see a scale on the sheet just like Table 6.1, but your legislator will likely have a different preference—again indicated by a gray cell—depending on his or her party and background.

Your Preference Sheet will similarly depict your legislator's positions on the other two issue areas. These areas relate to drilling on federal lands and the transfer of federal lands to state and local control. Table 6.2 portrays these issue areas as they will appear on your Preference Sheet.

The issue of drilling on federal lands refers to what, if any, restrictions the government should place on the extraction of petroleum resources from federal lands. The US government typically strikes a balance between leasing federal lands to oil and gas companies and preserving land for other purposes. Politicians disagree on just what this balance should be. Legislators who prioritize economic growth and job creation, even at the expense of the environment, will likely have their preferences on the higher end of Issue Two's scale. Our example legislator in Table 6.2 is at a 6, meaning that

TABLE 6.2 Issue Areas Two and Three

Issue Two—Drilling on Federal Lands

0	1	2	3	4	5	6	7	8	9
no drilling			reduce drilling			increase drilling			rampant drilling

Issue Three—The Transfer of Federal Lands

0	1	2	3	4	5	6	7	8	9
no transfer			limited transfer			extensive transfer			unlimited transfer

she wants to slightly increase drilling. Someone higher on the scale at a 9 would be so pro-drilling that they would put derricks atop Mt. Rushmore if there were oil in Washington's head. Conversely, a legislator at a 4 or below would decrease current levels of drilling on federal lands, and someone at 0 takes the hardline stance of ending it all together.

The third issue of transferring federal lands to state control is a Republican policy plank and originates in the Republican-controlled House's bill. Republicans argue that federal lands place an unfair burden on states and counties because local federal lands do not generate adequate tax revenue from economic activity. The GOP also argues that state and local officials know best how to manage lands in their area, so it would be better to transfer federal lands to their control. Someone at 1 or above on Issue Three's scale is in favor of at least some transfer of federal lands to state and local control, and a legislator at the high end of the scale would transfer whatever land states and counties would want to take. Democrats are not likely to agree with the transfer and some consider it a ploy to open up presently protected lands for exploitation by corporations. They would also be likely to note that states already receive compensation for federal lands within their borders in the form of Payments in Lieu of Taxes (PILTs) from the national government. Democrats would consequently sit low on the scale if not at 0. Pro-hunting legislators, including some Republicans, are also likely to oppose the transfer to some degree so that places for hunting and recreation are conserved. Our example legislator in Table 6.2 is at a 1 on the scale, and so she is open to only a minimal transfer of lands.

Each legislator in the game will have his or her own preferences, and together these preferences will vary all across the three issue area scales. This variety will make reaching a compromise set of values on the three issue areas for the final bill difficult. Compromise also works a little differently in a conference committee compared to a typical committee. Rather than needing a majority of everyone present, a conference committee needs any final proposal to be approved by both a majority vote of the Senators on the committee and a majority vote of the House members on the committee. A side effect of this is that it does not matter if there are unequal numbers of Senators and House members on the committee; what ultimately matters is achieving majority support within each group. Because the House is held by Republicans and the Senate by Democrats, most House members on the committee will be Republican and most Senators will be Democrats. This may mean that some bipartisan compromise will be necessary for the committee to pass a bill through both majorities.

Whatever the compromise, though, there will likely be some players opposing it due to the way scoring in the game works. In this game you score points based on how close the final result is to your legislator's preferences, which would be his or her ideal outcomes. For example, suppose that the committee passes a compromise with majorities agreeing to a 5 on the first issue, a 6 on the second issue, and a 4 on the third issue. We can state this more briefly as 5–6–4. Also suppose that we are determining the final score for our example legislator. Recall from Tables 6.1 and 6.2 that her preferences were 4–6–1. We start scoring with 30 possible points (10 from each issue) and deduct points based on how far the final result is from our example legislator's preferences. There is a distance of one between the final result on the first issue of the trust fund—5—and the legislator's preference of 4. This means we deduct 1 point on Issue One. On the second issue there is no distance—both are 6—so we deduct no points. On the third issue there is a distance of three, and we deduct 3 points. This results in deduction of 4 total points from the starting maximum of 30, leaving our example legislator with a score of 26.

Yet, if players' preferences are all over the three scales and they lose points based on how far the final result is from their preferences, how will majorities of players ever agree to support any set of numbers? The answer may come from two final mechanics in the game. The first is chits. Each legislator starts the game with five paper slips called chits, and they will serve as sort of currency in the game and translate into points in final scoring. In real-world terms, chits represent favors that legislators do for each other to get bills passed. That is, a legislator might say 'I'll vote your way on bill y if you vote my way on bill x.' A chit represents this sort of owed favor. In the game, you can use chits to pay other players to vote for a compromise bill you like. You can also accept chits from others in order to be paid for voting for a compromise that you perhaps do not like. This can be to your advantage because at the end of the game each chit is worth one point in final scoring. How you and other players exchange chits is up to you. We suggest treating them like a valuable currency. You may agree to hand over a chit payment only after, rather than before, a player has voted your way, for example.

The other remaining mechanic is missions. You will be able to select goals in the game, and they will reward points if you achieve them and cost you points if you fail them. You will be able to select as many of these goals as you wish, but be wary because the costs for not achieving them can add up and you cannot change your missions after you have selected them. Missions represent the dynamic influence of non-legislators on congressional negotiations. For example, in one mission you have the option to take up the interests of oil companies. If the final form of the bill increases drilling, you will gain points reflecting the campaign donations you will receive from the oil companies. If you fail, though, the oil companies may withdraw their support, costing you points. The missions that you may take are listed below:

- **The Dealmaker:** Power matters more to you than principle, and you like it when people owe you favors. Gain 10 additional points if you have ten or more chits at the end of the game. Lose 5 points if you have fewer than four chits at the end of the game.
- **The Obstructionist:** You do not want the committee to get anything done. Score 10 points if the committee fails to pass a conference report. Lose 5 points if the committee passes a conference report.
- **The Idealist:** You are a true believer in your party's goals. If you are a Republican, gain 10 points if a conference report passes with a value of seven or higher on issue area three; otherwise lose 5 points if you are a Republican. If you are a Democrat, gain 10 points if a conference report passes with a value of seven or higher on issue area one; otherwise lose 5 points if you are a Democrat.
- **The Oil Worker:** Drill, baby, drill! You know that if you help score a win for drilling, the oil corporations will support your reelection campaign. If the value on issue area two is six or higher in a passed conference report, gain 10 points. If the value

is lower than six or a conference report is not passed, lose 5 points.

- **The Braggart:** You have made some big promises about this bill to your constituents. They love it when you keep your promises but get angry if you let them down. Score 10 additional points if your point total from issue areas plus chits equals 20 or more at the end of the game. If you have fewer than 20 points from issue areas plus chits at the end of the game, lose 5 points.

- **The Tree Hugger:** You like the environment, and pro-environment interest groups will reward your continued support. Score 15 points if a conference report passes that has values higher than five on issue area one and lower than five on issue areas two and three. Lose 5 points otherwise, including if a conference report does not pass.

Sequence of Play

The game will consist mainly of negotiations and voting. However, before negotiations begin, there will be some preliminary phases in which you learn about your legislator, select your missions, and coordinate with other committee members. The game will then become more freeform, and it will be up to you, the players, to reach compromises and hold votes.

Phase One: Getting Started

At the start of the game, you will receive your Preference Sheet. It will have a short biography of your legislator at the top that should give you some perspective on why he believes what he does. It will also show the three policy issue areas presented in Tables 6.1 and 6.2 above with gray cells indicating your legislator's preferences.

There will be fourteen legislators total attending the committee. Four will be Senate Democrats. Two will be Senate Republicans. Five will be House Republicans. Three will be House Democrats. If there are more than fourteen players in your class, some people will likely end up sharing a legislator. In this case, the people sharing the legislator should identify one person to be the legislator, who will do any voting, leaving the remaining persons to take the role of staff members who can negotiate on the legislator's behalf during the game and help the legislator make the most advantageous decisions. If this legislator wins the game, so do his or her staffers.

The bottom half of your Preference Sheet will contain some items that you will cut or tear off. Immediately below the dotted line is a list of missions identical to the one above in this chapter. At the bottom of the page are five rectangles labeled as chits. First, carefully tear or cut away each of these chits. These will be your chits to use during the game. Second, fold along the dotted line, and then fold the page the other way again along the dotted line. Fold the page back and forth like this until a substantial crease forms in the page that lets you tear it easily. Or, if you have scissors, simply cut the page along the dotted line. Once the missions are removed from your legislator's preferences, select which missions you wish to pursue during the game by checking the boxes next to them. After also filling in your player and legislator names, return this portion of the page to your instructor so that he or she has a record of which missions you have chosen for the game. Note that you do not have to select any missions, but please return to the mission sheet to your instructor with your name(s) on it just the same.

Phase Two: Conferencing

During this phase, party members from the same house will meet to coordinate. So, House Democrats will meet together, as will House Republicans, Senate Democrats, and House Republicans. Use this time to work out a plan with other legislators and ask any remaining questions you have about the game. If other players cannot answer these questions, pose them to your instructor. Also use this time to talk about your legislators' biographies. You may pick up some talking points when hearing about the perspectives of other players who take the same positions as your legislator.

Phase Three: Negotiation

After your instructor calls conferencing to a close, whole-committee negotiations begin. How you play during this phase is up to you so long as you continue to abide by your instructor's expectations for classroom behavior. You can be a dealmaker, seeking out compromises and giving out chits to buy votes. You can be a holdout, withholding your support until you get what you want. If you have taken the obstructionist mission, you may even be a saboteur, trying to prevent successful votes so that you score the most points in the end. Regardless, you should follow your own instincts and play to win.

Phase Four: Voting

If you feel that you have a compromise set of values on the three issues that will pass, contact your instructor. Your instructor will call the class to order. She or he will then ask for a 'second,' that is, another legislator to support your call for a vote. If the motion to vote is seconded by another legislator, the instructor will ask all House members to vote on the compromise. Next, the instructor will ask all Senators to vote on the compromise. If a majority of House members (five) and a majority of Senators (four) vote for the compromise, it will pass out of the committee and play will move on to the last phase, scoring. If the vote fails, play will return to Phase Three.

Scoring

The game will reach this phase in one of two ways. The first is if a compromise successfully passes the two majority votes. In this case, players will score points based on how close their legislator's preferences were to the final outcome as described above in the gameplay section. They will also score points based on the number of chits they have (one point for each chit) and their successful missions. Players will lose points in accordance with any missions they fail.

The second way that scoring may begin is if time runs out before a compromise passes. In this case, players do not score points based on their legislator's preferences. Instead, they only score points from chits and missions. They may also lose points from any failed missions. All missions other than Dealmaker and Obstructionist automatically count as failed in this scenario.

Whichever legislator has the most points at the end of the game wins. If a legislator has staffers, the legislator and staffers all win or lose together. If you claim to win, your instructor may double check your score against any passed compromise, the mission sheet you submitted, and the chits you possess.

Debriefing

Describing What Happened

1. Did the game end in a successful bill, or did the bill fail to make it out of committee? How many unsuccessful attempts at passing a bill occurred before the game ended? What was the biggest difficulty in getting the votes?

2. How did players typically use their chits? Was exchanging chits a useful way to reach deals?

3. How did the missions you selected influence your voting behavior? If you did not select a mission, did it make reaching a compromise easier? Explain your answer.

4. Was it easier for some legislators to agree to a compromise? Why?

5. This game has few rules for reaching a compromise and largely lets players reach agreements as they see fit. Were there any informal rules that you and the other players followed? If so, what were they? If not, why do you think you did not need any?

Relating the Game to the World

6. When the houses of Congress are controlled by different parties, do you expect there to be fewer bills passed compared to when both houses are controlled by the same party? Why? How might conference committees help with this situation?

7. Given the wide range of individual legislators' preferences, what role might party leaders play in the lawmaking process to control or limit the influence of individual members of their parties?

8. How does the existence of issue linkage—tying future favors on another issue to the current issue—make compromise more or less difficult to achieve?

9. What is more important to individual legislators—party or personal ideology? Why?

10. Suppose that a legislator was following the obstructionist mission in real life. Why might they oppose the passage of a federal lands bill?

Thinking Deeply

11. Investigate a recent law passed by Congress. Research the conference committee membership. How did the final version differ from the House and Senate versions? Why?

12. How did the missions taken by players influence the outcome of the game? If there were no missions, how would the outcome have been different? What aspects of an individual legislator's decision-making process were not represented in the game? For instance, how might a legislator's reelection bid affect their behavior during the negotiations?

13. Analyze the environmental and economic impact of the final (proposed or successful) bill. What consequences would it have for parks and drilling?

14. How might personality interact with ideology and party to make compromise more or less difficult? In your answer, use yourself as an example and explain how your personality influenced your negotiation style.

15. Consider the shadow of a presidential veto. How does the president—who is not in the committee—influence lawmaking? How would a Republican president use this influence to affect negotiations over a federal lands bill? What about a Democratic president?

Creating New Ideas

16. Consider the three issue areas of the bill, and then add a fourth issue area. Describe this issue area and what would be on its scale. Why would this issue area be a good addition to the game? Does adding a fourth issue make compromise easier or more difficult?

17. Take the final bill (if the bill was unsuccessful, use the final proposed bill), and write it out into a formal bill in the style of a congressional law.

18. Write a journalistic narrative of the conference committee process. The narrative should be exciting and dramatize the ups and downs of the bill while also explaining the meat of the bill to the public and stakeholders (i.e., landowners and environmentalists). Consider the outlet for which you are writing: is it the *New York Times* or an industry journal like *Tri-State Livestock News* or an outlet like *Sierra* (the national magazine of the Sierra Club)?

19. Consider the bill from the position of a federal agency like the EPA. Now that the bill is law, how will you as this agency implement it? What steps will you need to take to be in compliance with the law and how might it affect your current operations? Develop a policy memo to the relevant agency head.

20. You are now the campaign manager for the legislator you represented in the game. Spin the outcome of the bill to support your candidate's bid for reelection. Develop the script for a thirty-second TV spot.

7

A Best-Case Scenario
A Game About the Supreme Court

In 1965, several students in the Des Moines Independent Community School District in Iowa decided on their own to wear black armbands to school to mourn casualties in the Vietnam War and call for a truce. They did not engage in any other display of protest at school or attempt to disrupt the school day. The school district responded by sending the students home, telling them to not return until they had removed the armbands. District administrators argued that the armbands were a danger to classroom order and discipline, and that consequently they were within their right to restrict the students' freedom to wear the armbands.

In this game, you will represent lawyers from Iowa's branch of the American Civil Liberties Union (ACLU). You have decided to represent three of the students—Mary Beth Tinker, John Tinker, and Christopher Eckhardt—in a court case against the school district. You are seeking an injunction that would prevent the school district from disciplining the students for wearing the armbands.

Your small team of ACLU lawyers will face key questions about the case as you play this game. Answering the questions correctly will help to move your case forward toward victory. Answering the questions incorrectly will set back your case. Answering incorrectly will not doom your case to failure, but you will score more points for answering correctly the first time you tackle a given question.

Aiding you in your journey toward legal success will be a game guide. This will be one of your fellow students who will not be playing the game but rather will be the one posing the legal questions that you and your teammates will have to answer. Your group's game guide is neutral and will not help you answer questions correctly.

We suggest listening carefully as your game guide reads aloud the set up to each question and the questions themselves. The questions, collectively, are designed to offer a sense of the weighty choices that civil liberties cases face and the winding journey that cases can go on as they make their way to the Supreme Court. We wish you well on this journey and luck in winning a victory for your clients.

Debriefing

Describing What Happened

1. Was there a question that was more difficult than the others? What made it stand out for you?

2. If you had to summarize your experience playing the game into three sentences, what would those sentences be?

3. Was there an answer to a question that you were surprised was right? What about it made it surprising?

4. What are some elements of the court system that the game does not cover?

5. What does the game tell you about the difficulties that a case faces as it tries to reach and win a majority at the Supreme Court?

Relating the Game to the World

6. If the Tinkers were in high school today, what do you think they would protest? How would they conduct their protest?

7. Think back to one of the 'wrong' answers in the game. What would have happened if the Tinkers had taken that route in real life?

8. In this game, your end goal was to win over at least five of the nine justices on the Supreme Court. How would arguments before the Court be different if there were only one justice? What about one hundred?

9. This game had you present particular statements in order to win justices to your side. Is this entirely realistic? How do you think justices make their decisions in the real world?

10. Identify another landmark Supreme Court case. What would be a 'necessary statement' that you would say would need to be made by the victors in that case?

Thinking Deeply

11. Disagreements related to the freedom of speech in schools happen often as administrators' needs for discipline conflict with students' desires for expression. Why do you think the Supreme Court specifically chose to hear *Tinker v. Des Moines* as opposed to other cases related to the first amendment in schools?

12. The ACLU has been behind many landmark Supreme Court cases. Briefly research the ACLU and explain why or why not you think it is an important organization for US society today.

13. Reaching the Supreme Court with a case can be a difficult, convoluted process. Should it be this difficult? Why or why not?

14. Identify an issue related to the freedom of speech that you think needs a ruling from the Supreme Court. What is this issue, why should it be the Court rather than Congress handling it, and why do past court cases not adequately address this issue?

15. What are the qualities that define a good Supreme Court justice? What are the qualities that are important in a lawyer who is arguing before the Court? Why are these different qualities important?

Creating New Ideas

16. Pretend that you are a journalist living in 1969 and that the decision in *Tinker* has just been announced. You are writing an article on the decision. What headline do you use for your article and what are three things that you would say as an evenhanded journalist about the significance of the decision?

17. Write a one-paragraph brief in which you take the side of the school district and explain why the students should not have won.

18. The US court system is adversarial with lawyers for both sides vigorously supporting their clients. Imagine a court system that was not adversarial and did not have lawyers arguing against each other. How would such a system handle complaints from plaintiffs? In your answer to this question, describe the court system and summarize an example of how a complaint would be handled in this system.

19. This game was written from the perspective of the plaintiffs' lawyers. Imagine, though, that it was written from the perspective of the defendants' lawyers. Write out a question that you think they would encounter as well as four answers and game guide responses to those answers indicating whether they are right or wrong and why.

20. Put yourself in the position of a Supreme Court justice. What are three questions you would ask the lawyers in *Tinker v. Des Moines* during oral arguments?

8

Agency and Oversight
A Game About Bureaucratic Politics

Overview

The federal government's powers are separated. A crucial point of separation is that the legislative branch creates laws while the executive branch implements them. This ensures that no one has total control over how laws work and is an important check against tyranny. However, the separation of powers does create conflicts. One of them is that the legislative branch and the executive branch often disagree over the creation and implementation of laws. This continual conflict manifests in the interactions between congressional committees, which oversee the implementation of laws, and executive agencies, which implement laws. In this game, you will play as either a committee or an agency, and your goal is to control the way laws are implemented. Yet, you will also retain the broader concerns of your branch of government and will have the opportunity to score points by influencing public perception on which branch of government should have the most control in executing laws. We wish you luck in coming out on top in this struggle, which is at the very heart of our national government.

Congress's power to monitor, influence, and review the work of federal agencies is called congressional oversight. It helps to ensure that the work of the executive branch's agencies is efficient, effective, and true to the intent of the law. Oversight is therefore crucial for preserving the health of the US's democracy. Yet, the oversight process is often contentious because congressional committees and federal agencies each have their own independent and sometimes conflicting desires.

Congressional committees want a variety of things out of the oversight process. Some of these objectives are relatively selfless. Committees may want to protect civil rights and liberties, publicize executive overreach, eliminate wasteful spending, gather information for future legislation, evaluate the effectiveness of government programs, or otherwise serve the public good. Their objectives may also be self-interested, though. Committees might wish to use oversight powers to eliminate projects they dislike, pressure for projects they do like, publicly embarrass ideological foes, or distract attention from other issues. Crucially, there is no guarantee that agencies will share any of these goals, creating the potential for conflict.

Indeed, agencies often have reason to resist congressional oversight. Some of this resistance is unavoidable; oversight by its very nature encroaches upon agency independence. However, agencies also have their own separate objectives that derive from presidential directives, their institutional mandate, their internal professional culture, lobbying by interest groups, their professional expertise, their relative insulation from the trends of national politics, and a variety of other sources. Some or all of these factors may end up incentivizing an agency to resist congressional oversight.

Should an agency wish to defy oversight, it has substantial capacity to do so. It must of course obey statutes, its own institutional mandate, and the Constitution, but it can also resist encroachment from Congress. One simple reason for this is that members of Congress cannot do everything. They do not have the time or the policy expertise to micromanage all the activities of an executive agency. Indeed, committees often rely on agencies for information about agency projects, meaning that an agency has a measure of control over what Congress knows and thinks about it. Altogether, this leaves bureaucrats with significant freedom to implement laws as they see fit and, if they wish, push back against a committee's wishes. If agencies truly feel under threat, they can also implement laws in ways that blatantly defy congressional interests, even though this risks sanctions from Congress. Whether used subtly or blatantly, though, agencies possess a meaningful capacity to resist the will of congressional committees.

This interplay between congressional oversight and agency independence is the topic of our game. You will play in a group with other players as either a congressional committee or an executive Agency. One of your goals, as either a Committee or an Agency, is to have your desires translated into policy. This takes place in the first phase of the game where you will negotiate with whichever institution you are not playing (i.e., Committees negotiate with Agencies and vice versa). Negotiating over actual policy implementation would be too complex for a game of this size, and so you will instead be negotiating over something simpler, a general resource called 'political capital.' In the context of this game, political capital is an aggregate measure of all the influence, goodwill, and reputation you gain from the negotiations. Basically, if you do well in negotiations, you get more political capital, bringing you closer to victory. Unfortunately, negotiations are zero-sum, meaning that the more capital you get out of the negotiations, the less your rival institution gets.

Just like in real life, Committees and Agencies will have different ways of trying to obtain what they want. For Committees, this entails the exercise of congressional oversight. Congressional oversight is represented in the game by Committees' power to offer terms in the negotiation, something that Agencies cannot do. Essentially, an offer of terms is a Committee's instructions to an Agency about how to implement a law, and it can only be given once in the negotiations. However, the offer will not actually include any policy details. Rather, its 'instructions' will be represented entirely by the political capital amounts that would result from the Agency following them. You are in effect negotiating over how much you benefit from the interaction rather than the details of policy implementation. The Committee can be generous and offer close to equal shares of political capital. It can also be greedy and try to keep the lion's share of the benefits for itself. It could also be giving and offer the majority of the benefits to the Agency.

The Agency, for its part, has the power to accept or reject a Committee's offer. If it accepts the offer, both groups gain the stated amount of capital. If the Agency rejects the offer, though, it gains half of the capital that the offer would have given it while the Committee gets no capital. This rejection represents the Agency's capacity to resist oversight, as discussed above. It can use this capacity to not follow the instructions of the Committee and instead implement the law in a way where it gets some of what it wants (half capital) and the Committee does not get any of what it wants (zero capital). This power of rejection gives the Agency an important tool for discouraging a Committee from giving an unreasonable offer.

After each negotiating phase, Committees and Agencies are left with whatever amounts of political capital they have gained in the game so far. They can then spend this political capital to influence the public's approval of congressional oversight, or ACO for short. Committees want the public to think that oversight is a good and necessary practice for keeping the executive branch in check, and they consequently use their influence (i.e., their political capital) to improve the public's approval of oversight. They might, for example, hold hearings that lambast the faults of an agency, boosting public favor for oversight of the executive branch. Agencies, of course, do not want this. They want the public to think that congressional oversight is meddlesome and a waste of time and resources, so they spend political capital to reduce the public's opinion of congressional oversight. In real-world terms, Agency officials might use press releases, public reports, testimony, and media interviews to boost public support for their work and portray oversight as partisan and counterproductive. At the end of the game, Committees will gain bonus capital if ACO is high while Agencies will gain bonus capital if it is low. It will be up to you to decide if it is better to save your political capital or invest it in adjusting public opinion in your favor.

Instructions and Rules

In this game, you will be divided into six groups. Three will represent Agencies (called A1, A2, and A3), and three will represent congressional committees (called C1, C2, and C3). The game will proceed through six rounds, with each round divided into two phases. In the first phase, Agencies and Committees will be paired together and given three minutes for (1) Committees to choose the instructions they want to give and (2) Agencies to accept or reject those instructions. In the second phase, both Agencies and Committees will have an opportunity to spend political capital they have earned to influence the public's approval of congressional oversight (ACO). The game ends after six rounds have been played, at which time final scores are tallied.

Gameplay

Setup

The instructor will have divided the room into six areas, providing some distinct space for Committees and Agencies to meet. Committees and Agencies receive labels: Committee 1, Committee 2, Committee 3, and likewise for Agencies. Each Committee and Agency appoints a spokesperson.

Phase One: Policy Directives

In the first phase of each round, Committees and Agencies are matched together. Committees stay put in predetermined locations in the room that are known to everyone. It is the responsibility of Agencies to come to them. Once the phase begins, Agencies and Committees have only three minutes to negotiate, so Agencies should be ready to move, and Committees should be ready to receive them. The pairings are determined by the round of play, which the instructor will update in the Public Space when each round begins. These are the pairings:

Round 1: C1 → A1; C2 → A2; C3 → A3
Round 2: C1 → A2; C2 → A3; C3 → A1
Round 3: C1 → A3; C2 → A1; C3 → A2
Round 4: C1 → A1; C2 → A2; C3 → A3
Round 5: C1 → A2; C2 → A3; C3 → A1
Round 6: C1 → A3; C2 → A1; C3 → A2

As soon as they are paired, Agencies should move to their assigned Committee for the round. Committees and Agencies are able to negotiate and discuss possible offers at this time. Members of both groups may talk to each other or whisper among themselves as strategy dictates. The Committee must by the end of the three minutes offer one of the four options listed below.

1. "Do what we say because we are the boss." If selected, the Committee gains 8 political capital; Agency gains 2 political capital.
2. "Please follow our preferred policy directives." If selected, the Committee gains 6 political capital; Agency gains 4 political capital.
3. "We are willing to concede that you raise some good points." If selected, the Committee gains 4 political capital; Agency gains 6 political capital.
4. "In the interest of simply getting something done, we concede to the Agency's wishes." If this is selected, the Committee gains 2 political capital; Agency gains 8 political capital.

When a Committee is ready to make its official offer, its spokesperson writes down the choice on a sheet of paper as well as the name of the current Committee–Agency pairing (for example, C1→A2) and hands it to Agency personnel. After a Committee has made an offer it cannot withdraw it; it is the only offer that it can make in that phase. Thus, some degree of discussion between the Committee and Agency prior to making an offer is probably a good idea.

Once an offer has been made, the Agency must make one of two responses:

1. The Agency may accept the offer by writing 'A' on the paper, then handing it to the instructor.
2. The Agency may reject the offer by writing 'R' on the paper, then handing it to the instructor.

At the end of the phase, the instructor updates the Public Space, which will look similar to the Public Space in Table 8.1. Where offers are accepted, the instructor records the increases in political capital for both Committee and Agency. Where offers are rejected, the Committee receives no political capital, and the Agency receives one-half of the political capital that it would have received had it accepted the offer.

TABLE 8.1 Public Space for Agency and Oversight

	Political Capital
Agency 1	
Agency 2	
Agency 3	
Committee 1	
Committee 2	
Committee 3	

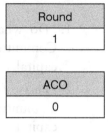

Round
1

ACO
0

If the instructor has not received a piece of paper from a Committee–Agency pairing by the end of Phase One, neither group in that pairing scores any points at all. Consequently, it is important that Committees not just make their offer within the time limit but also leave time for the Agency to select its response. Phase One ends when the instructor finishes tallying the political capital gains from the negotiations.

Note that during Phase One, members of Committees and Agencies are free to move around the room. They can observe other negotiations or have private conversations with members of other Committees and Agencies. Such communication might be useful in attempting to anticipate how other groups might score, which has implications for Phase Two, described below.

Phase Two: Public Posturing

In this phase, Committees and Agencies may expend accumulated political capital to influence the public's approval of congressional oversight (ACO). ACO is represented as a 20-point scale, where –10 indicates that the public does not approve of congressional oversight at all, and 10 indicates that the public loves it. It begins at 0 in the first round, which is the status quo. Agencies or Committees will score bonus points depending on what value ACO has at the end of the game. Table 8.2 below depicts these bonus points. As you can see, the number of points earned is significant, and so investing in ACO is an important strategic choice.

TABLE 8.2 Approval of Congressional Oversight Scale

8 to 10	Committees Earn 30 Political Capital
5 to 7	Committees Earn 20 Political Capital
4	Committees Earn 15 Political Capital
3	Committees Earn 10 Political Capital
2	Committees Earn 7 Political Capital
1	Committees Earn 3 Political Capital
0	
−1	Agencies Earn 3 Political Capital
−2	Agencies Earn 7 Political Capital
−3	Agencies Earn 10 Political Capital
−4	Agencies Earn 15 Political Capital
−5 to −7	Agencies Earn 20 Political Capital
−8 to −10	Agencies Earn 30 Political Capital

To invest in ACO, you will record your investments on slips of paper that your instructor will collect. Each group's slip should have the group's name on it (A2, C3, etc.). The instructor will then update the Public Space by reading each slip aloud, so that everyone is aware of who has invested, and then deduct three political capital from each investing group, adjusting the ACO score to its new value. The ACO score will decrease one for every Agency investor and increase one for every Committee investor. Note that groups may only invest once per turn.

The round ends after the ACO is updated in the Public Space. The game then moves on to the next round, in which new pairings of Agencies and Committees begin negotiations. After six rounds have been completed, the game ends and final scores are tallied.

Scoring

When the sixth round is completed, final scoring is calculated. The instructor adds any earned bonuses from the ACO to groups' political capital scores. The winner is the team or teams with the largest amount of political capital at the end of the game.

Debriefing

Describing What Happened

1. In what ways did Congress try to influence Agencies?

2. In what ways did Agencies assert their independence?

3. How often did Committees offer deals that were better for Agencies? How often did Agencies use their power to reject an offer?

4. What did you do to try to get what you wanted during negotiations? Were your efforts successful?

5. What is something that a different group did that surprised you during negotiations?

Relating the Game to the World

6. What is a reason why an Agency might reject an offer from a Committee in the real world?

7. Based on the way the game was played, would you say that Agencies or Committees are more powerful? Does this correspond to relations between both in the real world?

8. Political capital is used to represent a wide variety of powers and behaviors that political actors can use to get others to do what they want. Describe a current event in which you see political capital at work.

9. Identify an example of something done by a federal agency that you would want to be closely overseen by Congress. Identify another example of work done by a federal agency, one where you think Congress should take a hands-off approach.

10. Communication between Committees and Agencies is important. What types of things would you expect the EPA and the committee(s) overseeing it to say to each other?

Thinking Deeply

11. Suppose Congress is controlled by one party and the presidency by another. What sort of offers would the Committees give in

this situation? Would Agencies be more likely to reject? Why or why not?

12. What is the best winning strategy for Committees?

13. What is the best winning strategy for Agencies?

14. Did groups' strategies change over time? Why or why not?

15. Is it ever smart for Agencies to accept an offer that is better for the Committee? Why or why not?

Creating New Ideas

16. Choose a real-life executive agency. Examples include the Centers for Disease Control (CDC), United States Agency for International Development (USAID), the Bureau of Indian Affairs (BIA), the Food and Drug Administration (FDA), the Federal Emergency Management Agency (FEMA), and the National Institutes of Health (NIH). You may need to research this agency to answer the questions below.

    a. What is one reason why it is important for there to be oversight of this agency? What is one reason why it is important for this agency to be able to operate independently?

    b. What sort of professional culture do you think this agency has internally?

    c. If you were overseeing this agency, what rules would you want it to follow? Identify and explain two.

    d. What sort of oversight would this agency try to reject?

9

The Tragedy of the Lagoon

A Game About Resource Management

Picture a simple community of lagoon monsters. These intelligent amphibians have few tools and no government. They spend their mostly pleasant days fishing in their island lagoon. They sell their fish to neighboring communities for Clams, the local currency. In this game, you and your teammates will play as a family of these lagoon monsters. Your goal is to earn as many Clams as possible. However, you will face challenges that disrupt your idyllic existence. Squidfolk occasionally attack the lagoon and steal Clams from everyone. Fortunately, you can purchase insurance to protect yourself from these attacks. Your community's constant activity also drains resources and pollutes the lagoon's waters, and so you face the added challenge of keeping your waters safe for fishing. As you play, you will find that you have to balance earning Clams with protecting your family from these dangers. We wish you luck in finding the right balance.

Yet, what is the point of pretending to be preindustrial lagoon monsters, especially when this book is supposed to be about

American government? This game covers questions that are important across the social sciences, including American government. The very absence of government in the game invites questions about the proper role of government in society. In what ways would government help the lagoon monsters? In what ways would it hinder them? Which parts of lagoon monster society should government regulate, and which should it leave alone? This game also raises essential questions about collective action, that is, about getting different people to work toward a common good. These questions are encountered across American politics, including in the workings of interest groups, political parties, local politics, taxation, public resources, and government regulation. Your instructor will provide guidance regarding how this game fits into your course. This game serves as a tool for thinking about important issues in American politics even though these lagoon monsters are not in the US themselves. We hope that you enjoy this game and have a fruitful discussion after it is over.

Instructions and Rules

Gameplay

Teams

This game is played with players divided into five teams. Teams should be as close in size as possible. Each team represents a family of lagoon monsters struggling to survive in a lagoon shared with other lagoon monsters. Each team takes one action for *all* of its members each round, so each team should appoint a spokesperson to announce actions on the group's behalf. Students in teams are free to discuss possible actions among themselves throughout the game but should do so quietly to keep others from knowing what they might do. Teams, not individuals, are scored. If a team wins, everyone on that team wins. Different teams are referred to as 'Team One,' 'Team Two,' etc.

Rounds and Turns

The game is divided into rounds and turns. Each round, each team gets one turn where they take one action. Your team has thirty seconds to decide your action during your turn, but you should also have plenty of time to discuss quietly during other teams' turns. The possible actions are listed in bold and discussed below. After each team has taken its turn, the instructor updates information in the Public Space and the round ends. When the next round begins, the first team to take a turn changes to keep things fair for all teams. For example, if Team One went first in round one, Team Two would go first in round two, moving Team One to last in the order of play. This rotation continues each round, ensuring that every team gets a chance to go first.

Key Concepts: Clams, Fish, Water Quality

To succeed in this game, you should first understand three key concepts. First, Clams represent the currency used to buy and sell things in the lagoon. You can think of Clams as money. Clams are particularly important because they can determine who wins the game.

Second, Fish are, well, fish. You may sell Fish for Clams. However, there is a finite supply of Fish. If too many Fish are fished from the lagoon, then the local population of Fish dies out forever. This affects everyone because, when the lagoon is depleted of Fish, everyone is out of food and must import food from neighboring communities, which costs Clams. If there are no Fish in the lagoon and a team cannot afford to import new Fish, that team starves and loses the game.

Finally, Water Quality represents how habitable the water in the lagoon is. As time goes on, pollution from lagoon monsters lowers the Water Quality. When the Water Quality is entirely depleted, Fish begin to die, which will eventually cause teams to starve unless they can afford to import Fish from neighboring communities. The following section further describes how these important concepts interact, and how you may alter them.

Actions and Consequences

You must take one action each turn. Different actions do different things. Some actions help you earn Clams. Others cost Clams and protect you from dangers. You start with 5 Clams and your goal is to make as many Clams as possible without losing because of dangers, so choose your actions carefully!

Buy a Fishing Lure

Cost: 1 Clam

Gain: 1 Fishing Lure

The price of Lures increases as more Fishing Lures are purchased in a single round, reflecting principles of supply and demand. After every 2 Lures purchased, the price rises by 1 Clam. Lure prices reset to 1 after each round is played.

Go Fishing

Cost: 1 Fishing Lure

Gain: 3 Clams as a result of selling the fish

Fishing reduces number of Fish by 1. The population of Fish replenishes by 2 each turn and has a starting value of 5. If the population of Fish ever reaches 0, there is no chance for repopulation, so everyone runs out of local food and must begin buying food from neighboring communities, which costs 2 Clams at the end of each round.

Buy Squidfolk Attack Insurance

Cost: 1 Clam

Gain: 1 Insurance Policy

In the event of a Squidfolk attack, you can spend 1 Insurance Policy in order to lose 0 Clams instead of losing three. Squidfolk attack randomly. There is a 1-in-6 chance that Squidfolk will attack at the end of each round.

Improve Water Quality

Cost: 1 Clam

Gain: Water Quality improves by 1

Water Quality begins at 10 and decreases by 2 each turn to a minimum of 0. Water Quality cannot be improved after it hits 0. If the Water Quality marker ever hits 0, the fish population no longer replenishes and instead drops by 2 each round.

You win by having the most Clams when your instructor ends the game. Your instructor may pick a time or use a certain number of rounds to determine when the game ends, so pay attention. You lose the game early if you have 0 Clams and no way to gain more Clams (i.e., you have no Lures). You cannot go below 0 Clams, so if a Squidfolk attack would cause you to have a negative number of Clams, you just hit 0 instead.

The Public Space

Visualizing the Public Space for this game may help you understand how the game works. Please see Table 9.1. The Public Space will look something like this at the start of the game.

Sequence of Play

The Public Space is updated as the game is played in this way:

1. A round begins. The first team takes an action. Remember that the first team to act advances each round, such that Team One goes first in the first round, Team Two goes first on the second round, and so on.

   a. If a team has bought a Fishing Lure, the instructor adds a Lure to that Team's supply and subtracts 1 Clam. The number of Lures purchased that round, which is recorded in the Public Space, increases by 1. If two Lures have been purchased, the Lure Cost (also displayed in the Public Space) is increased to 2;

TABLE 9.1 Public Space for Tragedy of the Lagoon

Scorekeeping					Fish Population	Lures Bought This Round
First Team	Team #	Clams	Lures	Insurance	5	
*	Team 1	5	0	0		5
	Team 2	5	0	0	Water Quality	
	Team 3	5	0	0	5	Lure Cost
	Team 4	5	0	0		3 Clams
	Team 5	5	0	0		

if four Lures have been purchased, the Lure Cost is increased to 3.

b. If a team uses a Fishing Lure, the instructor adds 3 Clams and subtracts one Lure from the team's supply. The instructor also reduces the population of Fish by 1.

c. If the team buys Insurance, the instructor adds 1 Insurance Policy to the team's supply and subtracts 1 Clam.

d. If the Water Quality is improved, the instructor subtracts 1 Clam from the team's supply and increases Water Quality by 2.

2. Play passes to the next team listed in the Public Space and Step One (above) is repeated for that team. This continues until all teams have taken an action in the current round. Passing is not allowed.

3. The instructor rolls a die for a Squidfolk attack! On a 6, Squidfolk raid the lagoon for Clams.

a. If Squidfolk attack, any team with Insurance loses 1 Insurance Policy.

b. If a team does not have Insurance, the instructor subtracts 3 Clams from their supply.

4. The instructor updates the Public Space for the next round.

a. If the Fish supply is at 0, all teams must pay 2 Clams to purchase Fish from neighboring communities.

b. The instructor subtracts 2 from the Water Quality. If this brings Water Quality to 0, the instructor removes 2 Fish from the Fish population. Note that if Water Quality reaches 0, it can never be replenished.

c. If the Water Quality *and* Fish supply are greater than 0, the instructor adds 2 Fish to the supply.

d. If any team has 0 Clams and 0 Lures, they are eliminated from the game.

e. If any team has 0 Clams and there are no Fish left in the supply, they are eliminated from the game.

f. The instructor resets the Lure Cost to 1 and the Lures Purchased to 0.

g. The instructor designates that next team will start the next round.

5. Return to Step One in this list.

Scoring

The winning team is whichever team has the most Clams when the time designated by the instructor is reached (for example, the fifth round, or after forty minutes). The game can end early because only one team remains alive. If only one team is alive at the start of a new round, that team wins. If two or more teams are eliminated at the same time, and these are the last teams left alive, those remaining teams tie.

Debriefing

Describing What Happened

1. If you had to turn your experience playing the game into a three-sentence story, what would the story be?
2. Did groups tend to behave selfishly or unselfishly? How did your group behave?
3. Did the game feel different at the end compared to the beginning? Why or why not?
4. What do you think happened to the community of lagoon monsters after the events of the game?
5. Did you have an emotional reaction to any aspect of the game? If so, when and why?

Relating the Game to the World

6. Identify a real-world situation that is similar to that of the lagoon monsters. What is it, and why is it similar?
7. Identify two concepts that you have learned about in class that help to describe what happened in this game. What are they, and why do they help you to better understand the game?
8. To what extent did trust matter in this game? How does trust matter in politics?

9. Was there ever a point in the game where you felt that you had no choices? Provide a real or fictional example, of your choice, where people had no choices in the situation they were in.

10. For each of the four points below, you will identify a product, service, or resource that functions like one in the game.

    a. Name a good that works like Lures, which are consumed upon use and can be withheld from people who do not pay for them.

    b. Name a good that functions like Fish, which are in finite supply but which anyone can try to obtain.

    c. Name a good that is like Insurance in the game, which can be sold in unlimited supply but only to those who pay.

    d. Name a good similar to Water in the game, which is in limited supply and which anyone can use (but which also, perhaps, can be polluted or harmed).

Thinking Deeply

11. What was the best strategy for winning, and what does this say about how communities like this can prosper or suffer?

12. After playing this game, do you think that cooperation in an environment where essential resources are declining is possible? Why or why not?

13. What would happen if the number of teams increased or decreased? Would cooperation be easier or more difficult to achieve?

14. What would happen if the teams were separated and could not see each other during the game?

15. Imagine that just you played this game with members of your immediate family (or your closest relatives). How might the outcome of the game change?

Creating New Ideas

16. Suppose that the lagoon monsters create a government. What are three laws that this government should enact to make the lives of lagoon monsters better?

17. Write a seven-line poem about the life of a lagoon monster. It does not have to rhyme.

18. If you were to redesign the game to make it more likely that teams contribute to improve Water Quality, how would you change the game? What would this adaptation look like in the real world?

19. Is it possible to establish a Utopia in which humans use their environment without slowly destroying it? What would this Utopia look like?

20. Prepare a statement to read to the other teams to compel them to cooperate. How would you convince others to contribute to the public welfare?

10

The People Have Spoken

A Game About Interest Groups and Messaging

Game Overview

Interest groups play an important role in any democratic political process. They are one way that individual interests can be aggregated into larger messages that can resonate across the political world. Interest groups adopt various strategies to fulfill their goals. Some of these relate to money: through donating money to politicians or Political Action Committees, a well-funded interest group can hold a lot of sway. However, this game focuses on another side of interest groups: how they craft and deliver messages to *persuade* the public that their message is right and thereby promote fundraising, volunteers, a larger membership base, and the exertion of political pressure on politicians. Public opinion is shaped and molded by a lot of different inputs. Can you make yours matter the most?

In this game, your team will take a leadership role in a particular interest group and will be asked to confront various challenges on a tight timetable. Your goal is to articulate the goals and messages of your group to the class in the clearest and most interesting manner;

to succeed, you must keep in mind that political messages can be as much substantive as theater. As you compete to gain support for your desired policies, you will have to think quickly, consider the mood of the judges (who comprise the American citizenry), and even contemplate how popular culture can be harnessed to sell people on political messages.

Instructions and Rules

Setup

1. When the competition begins, you will be assigned to one of the following interest groups. They are:

   - The Sierra Club, an interest group devoted to protecting the environment.
   - The National Rifle Association, an interest group devoted to the protection of 2nd Amendment rights.
   - The American Civil Liberties Union, an interest group devoted to protecting civil rights and liberties of citizens.
   - The AARP, an interest group devoted to protecting the rights of the elderly.
   - The American Federation of Labor and Congress of Industrial Organizations, an interest group devoted to forwarding the political agenda of unionized workers.

2. Your group will either be given ballots by your instructor, which you will use to vote for the best proposals throughout the game, or you may be instructed to rip up sheets of paper to create your own ballots.

First Round

As soon as you are given your interest group and decide who will be addressing the class, a member of your group must complete two tasks on the Public Space. The instructor will determine how long the round will last and will make this publicly known. When time expires, you must stop recording information on the Public Space, so gauge your time carefully.

First, before sending anyone to the Public Space, your group will develop a one sentence mission statement describing the aims of your interest group. For example, if your interest group happened to revolve around the defense of Pink Floyd's music in popular culture, it might be, "to protect and preserve the music of Pink Floyd." You should not use the actual mission statement of the organization you are given. This is your message to create.

Next, your group should invent a symbol that somehow represents your group and its aims. This symbol can be anything, but it must be drawn and contain very little, if any, text. The idea is to visually represent your group's goals in a way that an average citizen could understand with just a second or two of review.

Once you have finished thinking about your contribution, send a member of your group to the Public Space to write your group name, motto, and symbol on the top of the Public Space. These will persist throughout the game to keep your fundamental goals continually visible. Don't take up too much space, because all groups will need to place this same information on the top of the Public Space. When completed, the Public Space should look something like Figure 10.1. The idea is to give each group a distinct place to stand when presenting information, as well as equal space to record additional information.

When the instructor calls 'time,' a member of each group should be standing near that group's contribution. Each group will then be given some time (determined by the instructor) to explain their slogan and symbol. The instructor will cut you off if you go over your allotted time. The Sierra Club will start, followed by the NRA, and so on.

After these presentations, all students secretly vote for whichever combination of slogan and symbol is the 'best.' 'Best' is a subjective

The Sierra Club	NRA	ACLU	AARP	AFL-CIO

Figure 10.1 Public Space for The People Have Spoken

judgment, but, in essence, you must choose which of the messages is the most effective in conveying its intended message. You will write this on one of the ballots given to you at the start of the game. You may not vote for your own group, and you should not vote strategically (for the worst proposal, for example, or collude to spread your votes out evenly so as to disperse its effect). You will also vote individually, without conferring with your group members. Please play honorably and vote for whichever proposal you believe is best at conveying its message. Again, you cannot vote for your own group!

The instructor takes all the ballots. The instructor will count them during the next round, while groups are discussing their responses to scenarios (see below), and place the vote totals on the Public Space beneath the group name, motto, and symbol.

Additional Rounds

All further rounds are played in a similar way, but with a twist: the instructor will announce a scenario, and all groups will be asked to create, craft, articulate, or decide something, and then present it in front of the class. Again, the goal of each group is to most clearly and interestingly articulate the goals of their particular interest group. The instructor will determine how much time the group has to consider instructions and how much time spokespeople will have to present results.

For example, a scenario might be:

Congress has completed a draft of its annual budget. However, both the House and Senate are still in negotiations regarding the final version. This is the last opportunity for citizens to be heard. Your job is to develop a strategy to advocate for your interest group by creating political pressure or public awareness regarding why your interest should receive special attention in the bill.

After the instructor calls 'time,' a group member will stand in front of the Public Space and present what the group has created. It is crucial to be fast, accurate, and concise, as you will be cut off if you fail to complete your presentation in the allotted time.

The first group to present in each round becomes the last group to present in the next round so that no group enjoys more time to think than any other. For example, because the Sierra Club goes first in the opening round, the NRA goes first in the next round, followed by the ACLU, and so on, so that the Sierra Club is the last to present. The instructor will keep track of the first group to present in any given round in the Public Space, near the name of your interest group, with a star or some other designator. When all are completed, spokespersons return to their seats.

At this point, all students vote for whichever interest group they feel best fulfilled the prompt or challenge issued by the instructor. Again, keep in mind that you cannot vote for yourself, and that the objective of these challenges is to communicate information about interest groups in the most meaningful and interesting way.

Scoring

At the end of the game, whoever has the most points in the Public Space wins the competition.

Debriefing

Describing What Happened

1. Which interest group do you believe did the best job getting their point across?

2. How would you evaluate the performance of your team (or, if playing alone, your interest group) in this game? What did you do well, and what did you do poorly?

3. What was your favorite proposal or performance conducted by your team during the game?

4. What was your favorite proposal or performance conducted by another team during the game?

5. Of all the interest groups showcased here, which would you like to join, and why?

Relating the Game to the World

6. Identify a current event from the last month. How would your interest group have reacted to this current event in a way that would have furthered its goals?

7. Interest groups often rate politicians based on how much the group likes the politician's actions. Choose one of the following presidents—Franklin Delano Roosevelt, Richard Nixon, Ronald Reagan, or the current president—and rate this president between 0 (awful) and 10 (amazing) based on how much you think your interest group would like this president. Explain your answer with reference to particular things that this president has done.

8. Suppose that have the opportunity to change your interest group's mission statement and symbol to better reflect what your group did during the game. What, if any, changes would you make? Explain your answer.

9. Lobbying politicians is an important activity for an interest group like yours. Suppose you could alter a key part of your interest group, such as its name, membership requirements, or purpose. What would you change about your interest group in order to make politicians more interested in listening to your group during lobbying? Explain your answer.

10. Interest groups often provide material benefits (magazines, discounts, tote bags, etc.) to their members. What is a material benefit that you think your interest group should offer to attract new members?

Thinking Deeply

11. Throughout the game, you were asked to evaluate the 'best' proposal. This was clearly a suggestive choice. Think carefully about why you voted the way you did, and explain your logic. What made something 'the best'? How does this relate to how the public receives political messages?

12. Conversely, you likely encountered some proposal that you thought was terrible. Without naming names, identify what made it unappealing. Explain why some messages fell flat, and come up with one example of a political advertisement in the real world that felt equally lousy to you.

13. Do you think this game does a good job of modeling how interest groups communicate in the real world? Why or why not?

14. Did you at any point use deception in your presentations, and if so what form did it take? Does the use of such deception (even if you didn't do it yourself) pose a danger to American democracy?

15. Should interest groups have such freedom to influence society? Is this consonant with the fundamental premise of American democracy?

Creating New Ideas

16. Consider your favorite proposal or presentation from the game. If you had an unlimited amount of time to develop the idea, what would you change to make it better?

17. Interest groups often send out 'urgent' emails to supporters requesting donations. Imagine that a candidate that your group likes is tied in the polls with her opponent a month before the election. Write up the text of an email to send to your group's supporters that will create enough panic or enthusiasm in them to donate money.

18. Develop three scenarios, drawn from current political and social situations, that could be used if this game were played again tomorrow.

19. Browse a social media site like Facebook or Tumblr. Note any advertisements from an interest group. How would you alter these messages to be more effective?

20. Imagine the most appalling, offensive, and useless ad for your interest group. Draw this train wreck.

11

Game Goulash

Overview

This chapter presents a set of games that can each be played in under thirty minutes. Like the games appearing earlier in this text, these shorter exercises each portray important concepts in the study of US government. Information Disclosure covers the competition between organs of the US government over intelligence in the wake of a national tragedy. Ironing the Triangle is about the mutually beneficial relationships between interest groups, federal agencies, and congressional committees. No Way or the Freeway has players working through the dynamics of federalism and the various levels of American politics on a giant tic-tac-toe board. Past the Post helps players to experience how different electoral systems can yield different electoral outcomes. Zombie Caucus puts players in the position of Iowa caucus-goers if dead presidents had risen from the grave and run for office again. We hope that you enjoy these games and wish you luck in winning them!

Information Disclosure

Background

Government organizations are constantly collecting intelligence about threats at home and abroad, including domestic and foreign terrorists. However, the various agencies that collect this information do not always share it with one another. This can be for legal purposes (the FBI is generally not privy to national security concerns that do not take place on US soil or directly involve US citizens), inter-agency rivalries (as the 9/11 Commission concluded was a contributing factor to the hijackings of September 11, 2001), or because their level of confidence in information is low.

Politicians have uneven access to this information. This could be due to Beltway politics, interpersonal relationships, or simply because they are not listening or asking the right questions. Additionally, upon receiving intelligence, civilian politicians must make a decision whether or not to disclose this information to the public. Disclosing information that is correct can help establish the power and credibility of a politician or group of politicians before the American people; disclosing incorrect information based on fragmented intelligence—such as the claim that weapons of mass destruction were present in Iraq in 2003—can be embarrassing and harmful.

In this game's scenario, a small nuclear weapon has been detonated in Houston, Texas. The weapon is weak by nuclear standards—about four times the destructive power of the bombs that struck Hiroshima and Nagasaki near the end of World War II. The American public is clamoring for answers, and different groups in government (the Presidential Administration, the Senate Intelligence Committee, the House Intelligence Committee, and the Department of Homeland Security) want to give it to them to increase their standing and stature in Washington. However, they do not want to be wrong. Who can piece together what happened first and disclose it to the public?

Gameplay

Before the game starts, the instructor will divide students into four groups, which represent the Presidential Administration, the Senate Intelligence Committee, the House Intelligence Committee, and the Department of Homeland Security. The instructor will arrange twenty slips of paper in a common space in plain view. Each slip represents a piece of relevant intelligence collected by an intelligence-gathering apparatus such as the Central Intelligence Agency, the National Security Agency, or military intelligence. Because these agencies are often guarded in releasing information, these 'clues card' slips of paper are fragmented and not in any systematic order. Some are more valuable than others. Collectively, they make up a sort of jigsaw puzzle that can enable a group to piece together what happened and then release the information to the public.

Play starts with the Presidential Administration and proceeds in an order designated by the instructor. Every group gets one turn, after which play passes to the next group. When all groups have taken their turns, play returns to the Presidential Administration.

On each turn, a group may perform one of the following three actions:

- **Request Information:** The group holds a hearing, demands a briefing, or otherwise requests information from one intelligence-gathering apparatus. Draw one 'clue card.'
- **Share Information:** The group may share the contents of one of their 'clue cards' with another group, in return for the other group sharing one of its cards. Both groups must agree to the exchange. If the exchange is agreed-upon, both groups must share cards that the other group has not seen before. This is done privately, such that other groups cannot see the contents of the cards. Groups are free to record the information that they share.
- **Disclose:** If a group thinks that it has unveiled the perpetrator of the attack, it may disclose this information to the public. If correct, the group wins; if incorrect, the group is eliminated from the game. The 'clue cards' are returned to the central depository, placed face down, and randomized.

As mentioned in the actions list above, the winning group is the one that correctly guesses the identity of the perpetrator of the attack. Be careful in your guessing, though, because if you choose to Disclose and are wrong, your group is eliminated from the game. We wish you luck in this race to decipher intelligence.

Questions

1. Rivalries between politicians and bureaucrats can often weaken the potential for good governance and damage our national security. Where did you observe such rivalries in this game? What could be done to prevent it?

2. In a democracy, the public has a right to know certain information. However, the irresponsible release of information can create a public outcry for improper foreign intervention or domestic action. Was the release of information in this scenario too cautious, or reckless?

3. In the race to disclose information, do you think that politicians and bureaucrats are more motivated by public safety or their own political fortunes?

Ironing the Triangle

The concept of the iron triangle shows how different elements of government and society mutually support each other. In this game, you will play as one of the three 'corners' to the iron triangle, either as an interest group, a federal agency, or a congressional committee. When it is your turn, you will be able to award points to the other corners in your triangle or to yourself, as laid out below under your corner's 'actions.' Your goal is to score the most points, but what is the best way to do it? Which action will you choose on your turn? What will you do to help the other corners choose to give points to you on their turns?

Please follow your instructor's directions for getting into groups, taking turns, and scoring points. Once you have selected or been assigned a corner of the triangle, familiarize yourself with that corner's choices as listed below. When it is your turn, you will select one of those choices, and then your group will be ready for the next turn. Make sure you keep track of your points and good luck!

Interest Group Actions

1. **Support Congresspersons for Reelection**: The Congressional Committee gains 3 points. It becomes the Committee's turn.

2. **Lobby Congress to Support Federal Agency**: The Federal Agency gains 3 points. It becomes the Agency's turn.

3. **Withhold Support by Running Ads Against the 'Washington Establishment'**: The Interest Group gains 1 point. It remains the Interest Group's turn.

Federal Agency Actions

1. **Lower Regulation for Interest Group's Supporters:** The Interest Group gains 3 points. It becomes the Interest Group's turn.
2. **Carry Out Laws the Way Congresspersons Prefer:** The Congressional Committee gains 3 points. It becomes the Committee's turn.
3. **Withhold Support by Implementing Laws Your Own Way:** The Federal Agency gains 1 point. It remains the Federal Agency's turn.

Congressional Committee Actions

1. **Give More Funding to Federal Agency:** The Federal Agency gains 3 points. It becomes the Federal Agency's turn.
2. **Provide Favorable Oversight and Laws for Interest Group's Supporters:** The Interest Group gains 3 points. It becomes the Interest Group's turn.
3. **Withhold Support by Holding Public Investigations Into the Other Parts of the Triangle:** The Congressional Committee gains 1 point. It remains the Committee's turn.

Questions

1. Were you taking the same actions at the start of the game compared to the end? Why or why not?
2. How was the game similar to iron triangle relationships in the real world? In what ways are actual relationships between Congress, federal agencies, and interest groups more complicated than the game portrays?
3. Are iron triangle relationships between Congress, federal agencies, and interest groups good or bad for democracy? Should interest groups have this much influence? Explain your answers.

No Way or the Freeway

Federalism in the US is simple in principle. The Constitution identifies powers that belong specifically to the federal government, powers that are reserved for the states, and powers that are shared concurrently by both the national and state governments. In practice, however, federalism is messy. Federal, state, and local agencies interact with each other and with other actors like courts, legislators, governors, lobbyists, corporations, and city councils in convoluted ways.

The game you are about to play seeks to portray the complicated nature of federalism in the US. It is loosely based on California's decades-long struggle to extend the 710 Freeway through cities like Alhambra, Pasadena, and South Pasadena in the San Gabriel Valley. The California Department of Transportation (also called Caltrans) and the Los Angeles County Metropolitan Transportation Authority (known simply as Metro) have collaborated to push forward proposal after proposal to build this freeway connection. However, at federal, state, and local levels, this project has been opposed and delayed again and again, demonstrating how the different levels of government in the US's federal system can interact in surprisingly extensive ways.

Gameplay

The game presents the project's struggles in the format of a giant tic-tac-toe board. We encourage you to look at this board now if possible so that these instructions make more sense. The board has nine sections in a 3×3 format. Within each section there are nine squares, again in a 3×3 format. This means that the board effectively has nine tic-tac-toe games that are themselves arranged into a larger tic-tac-toe game.

Your goal is to win this larger tic-tac-toe game. But how do you do that? Gameplay proceeds like a normal game of tic-tac-toe where you and your opponent take turns marking individual squares on the game board. You can win a section by winning the game of tic-tac-toe within it, that is, by marking three squares in a line vertically, horizontally, or diagonally. Your larger goal is to win three sections in a line. If you do this, you win the game.

As you play, read aloud the text in each square you mark. The text will relate to law, politics, or society at the national, state, or local level, depending upon where the square is on the game board. Each piece of text portrays an event that obstructs work on the freeway project. The player using Os as their symbol represents a consortium of interests who oppose the project. They, of course, want these events on the game board to occur. Circling an event represents them causing this disruptive event to happen. If this player is able to cause a coordinated set of these events to occur across the three levels of government (i.e., claiming three sections vertically or diagonally) or across one entire level of government (i.e., claiming three sections horizontally), this player wins. Conversely, the player using Xs as their symbol represents a group of people and institutions who want the freeway project to go forward. This player's goal is to stop the project from being derailed by preventing these disruptive events from happening, by putting Xs on them. If the player can claim three sections in a line, they effectively safeguard the project from disruption.

Questions

1. What does the game say about the complicated nature of federalism in the US?
2. The game treats all of the events on the board as being roughly equal to each other in terms of potential impact. Is this realistic? Why or why not?
3. If your game had a winner, look at the squares that the winner of your game used to win. How might the combination of these events have helped cause the project to go forward or fail? If your game was a tie, which squares were crucial for creating this stalemate? Could these events have been equally crucial in real life? Why or why not?

Past the Post

Round One: Plurality

Imagine that the United States has lost its collective mind and passed a Constitutional amendment saying that only celebrities can be elected to Congress. As a result, celebrities have moved around the country to different congressional districts in order to run for office. In this game, you will play a US citizen voting for celebrities and, if you desire, betting on who will win in your district.

Your instructor will list three celebrities running in your district. One is from the Famous for Being Famous (FBF) party. This party has candidates who are mainly known for their media presence and not for their accomplishments. Another candidate is from the I've Got Something to Say About That (IGSSAT) party, which runs celebrities who are always offering their opinions on politics and social issues. A third candidate is from a 'third party,' the Get Real (GR) party. This party only runs reality TV stars as its candidates.

Step One: Bet

Who do you think will win? You have two points with which you can bet in a manner of your choosing. That is, you could bet two points on one candidate, one each on two candidates, none on anyone, etc. If the candidate on which you bet wins, you double your bet. So, for example, if you bet one point and win, you keep that point and gain another one. If the candidate loses, you lose all the points that you bet on that candidate. You record these bets on your own paper and keep track of them yourself.

Step Two: Vote

Which candidate wins? Cast a vote for the celebrity you like the best (or dislike the least). Your instructor will likely conduct the vote by raised hands. Record your winnings or losses from your bets.

Step Three: Discuss

1. Only one candidate was elected despite the fact that some voters (presumably) did not support that candidate. Is this result fair? Why or why not?

2. One candidate came in third. Did this candidate's level of success help to explain why third-party candidates struggle so much in the US? Why or why not?

3. Why did you bet the way that you did? Did it make sense to split your points and bet on more than one candidate?

Round Two: Closed List Proportional Representation

It is now two years later, and it is time for new election. However, another amendment to the Constitution has come into effect. The US has decided to begin using a closed list proportional representation (CLPR) system for electing representatives to Congress. Under this system, each Congressional district will elect three representatives to Congress rather than just one.

The way you vote is also different under this new system. Instead of casting a vote for persons, you will be casting a vote for a party. If a party wins one seat, the first candidate on a list of candidates for that party gets elected. If the party wins two seats, the second candidate on the list also gets elected, and so on. In order to get one of the seats, a party will have to earn a set minimum number of votes, called a quota. This quota value will vary depending upon the size of your class, and so it is something that your instructor will need to calculate and share with your class.

Your instructor will provide your class with the party lists for each party running in the election. This cycle, the parties include FBF, IGSST, GR, and one new party, Triple Threat (TT). This party lists candidates who are known for doing at least three things well, such as singing, dancing, and acting.

Step One: Bet

Which parties are likely to get a seat or seats? In this round, you again gain two points at the start of the round, which you add to your total of points from the previous round. You can bet all of your points as you choose among the four parties (all on one party, divided among the parties, none on any party, etc.). If a party on which you bet wins a seat, you double your points (so, if you bet one, you get two points back). You triple your points if the party wins two seats and quadruple them if it wins three seats. If a party on which you bet gains no seats, you lose whatever points you bet.

Step Two: Vote

Vote on the party that you like the best. You might also consider the candidates who are at the top of each party's list and would get elected if the party wins a seat. Note that even though there are now three seats in your district, you still only get one vote.

Step Three: Discuss

1. In this round, the number of parties grew in response to the number of seats available. Do you think this is realistic? Why?

2. Were the results of this election more or less fair than in the first round? Why?

3. Was your betting strategy different because there were more seats? Why or why not?

Step Four: Tally Points

The winner of the game is the person with the most points. Do the points matter? Not at all.

Zombie Caucus

Zombies walk the earth! It has not been much of an apocalypse, though. The dead rose from their graves, and, instead of wanting to eat brains, they just desired to go about life as they used to live it. This includes undead US presidents wanting to be president again. Today the animated remains of Ulysses S. Grant, Grover Cleveland, Millard Fillmore, Herbert Hoover, and many other former presidents are shambling along the campaign trail, giving speeches with drawn-out vowel sounds, and trying to drum up support for their postmortem presidential candidacies.

Even though all undead presidents are eligible to be commander in chief again thanks to a contentious Supreme Court ruling, most of them have not gained enough support to be serious contenders in the Iowa caucuses. Only a handful will be considered in your precinct for the Democratic and Republican caucuses. Iowa's first-in-the-nation status in the primary season gives you, an Iowa voter, a unique influence on which zombie will become the next president. Which dead president will you choose?

Round One: The Republican Caucus

You are a caucus-goer for the Republican Party. You are in a large room with other Republican voters (i.e., your classmates). After listening to some speeches supporting the various candidates, it is time to vote.

Step One: Predict

A caucus official (your instructor) will post a list of Republican candidates competing for delegates in Iowa. Predict which candidate will get the most votes in your precinct. Write down your guess. This step is not part of the actual caucus and occurs for the sake of the game.

Step Two: Vote

Write the name of the candidate you support the most on a piece of paper. Submit it to the caucus official. Congratulations, you have successfully voted in the Republican caucus!

Step Three: Check Results Against Predictions

Was your prediction about the winner correct? If so, score one point. If not, score no points.

Round Two: The Democratic Caucus

You are a caucus-goer in the Democratic Party. You are in a large room with other Democratic voters, some of whom you recognize from your neighborhood. A caucus official begins to direct you through the several steps in the caucus voting process.

Step One: Predict

The caucus official will list candidates for the Democratic Party nomination under consideration in your precinct. Which candidate will get the most delegates? Make a prediction by writing down your guess on a piece of paper. This prediction step is not part of the actual caucus and occurs for the sake of the game.

Step Two: Move

The official will also designate areas around the room for supporters of each candidate to gather. If you find that you support one candidate over all the others, go to that candidate's location now. If you are as yet undecided, go to the location for undecided voters.

Step Three: Caucus

Use this time to win support for you candidate or, if you are still undecided, to choose a candidate. You are free during this stage to mingle about the room and converse with the supporters of various candidates. This is a key opportunity to persuade other voters to your side, something that does not happen during voting in primaries.

Step Four: Determine Viability

At this point, the caucus official counts the number of supporters for each candidate. Any candidate with less than 15% of the voters in attendance becomes non-viable and is out of consideration. The supporters of such candidates must now find a viable candidate to support.

Step Five: Caucus Again

This stage repeats Step Three. Supporters of a viable candidates should again try to recruit more voters for their candidate, particularly the people who are still undecided and the former supporters of non-viable candidates. The final vote will occur after this stage, so this is your last chance to persuade other voters (or be persuaded) to support a particular candidate.

Step Six: Award Delegates

Delegates will now be awarded to each candidate based on the number of supporters they have. Your precinct is electing four delegates. This means that the equation for awarding delegates to candidates is as follows:

(Number of People in a Candidate's Group × 4) / (Number of Present Eligible Voters) = Number of Delegates Awarded to Candidate

In cases where the number resulting from this equation has a decimal, decimals of .5 of higher should be rounded up, and decimals lower than .5 should be rounded down.

Step Seven: Check Results Against Predictions

Were you correct in your prediction from Step One? If so, score a point. If you were not correct, score no points.

Scoring

The player(s) with the most points from predictions win(s).

Questions

1. What made it difficult or easy to predict the winning candidate in the two caucuses?
2. Did the method of voting in the Democratic caucus cause you to change your mind about a candidate? Why or why not?
3. Which method of voting do you think is more democratic? Why?

Index